The Intentional Executive

A Purpose-Driven Playbook to Transform Your
Leadership, Your Team, and Your Results

By

Melissa Norcross, PhD, MBA and
Patrick Farran, PhD, MBA

The Intentional Executive: A Purpose-Driven Playbook to Transform Your Leadership, Your Team, and Your Results

Paperback ISBN: 979-8-89576-083-3

Published by:

Dedication

To my mom, Dr. Carol Farran, who taught me the true meaning of purpose-driven leadership long before I had the words to describe it.

One of my first jobs, at the age of 10, was coding my mom's dissertation on the topic of hope. She was an exceptional boss who set a high bar for excellence that would influence my entire professional journey. Alongside her, I witnessed her unwavering work ethic, remarkable tenacity in the face of challenges, and passionate dedication to helping others.

Her pioneering research transformed healthcare approaches for caregivers of individuals with Alzheimer's disease. With over 100 publications to her name, she instilled in me a deep appreciation for the power of the written word. But her impact on me went far beyond her professional accomplishments, as she patiently reviewed countless papers and taught me that writing isn't just about conveying information. She taught me that writing is about connecting with others in meaningful ways. Her thoughtful feedback shaped me as both a writer and a thinker.

Mom, though Alzheimer's has cruelly taken your ability to read these words, your spirit infuses every page of this book. Your commitment to excellence, your genuine care for others, and your quiet determination to leave the world better than you found it remain my North Star. This book is dedicated to you, with profound gratitude for showing me that purpose is not just something we talk about. Purpose is something we live.

—Patrick

Acknowledgement

As we gathered best practices, we found ourselves distilling insights from hundreds of sources. We drew upon published books and articles, executive interviews, and our own experiences working alongside leaders. In the process, we had a generous circle of co-authors and thought partners guiding us through the journey. We wish to thank all of those who contributed to this journey.

We are also profoundly grateful for the unwavering support of our family and friends. Their patience, encouragement, and help mean more than words can express.

Thank you all.

—Melissa and Patrick

Table of Contents

Recognize the Power of Mindset

"The purpose of life is not to be happy. It is to be useful, to be honorable, to be compassionate, to have it make some difference that you have lived and lived well." —Ralph Waldo Emerson

It's Sunday night. Another week looms ahead with impossible deadlines, competing priorities, and a team looking to you for direction. The weight of leadership feels heavier than ever. Sound familiar?

Today's leaders face unprecedented challenges. They're required to do more with less amid extraordinary disruptions—from technological upheavals like automation and AI to geopolitical uncertainties to fundamental shifts in how and where work gets done. Many organizations have recently cut 20-40% of their workforce, leaving leaders with fewer resources but higher expectations. They must navigate these choppy waters while maintaining team morale, driving innovation, and delivering results.

Their teams are also feeling the pressure. Employees are grappling with concerns about job security, questioning the long-term viability of their careers, and are often hesitant to take risks in an unstable environment. Meanwhile, leaders have less support than ever, with fewer peers to lean on and reduced organizational resources to tap into.

Purpose-driven leaders don't just survive these challenges - they transform them into opportunities for extraordinary impact. They build resilient teams, create sustainable success, and find deep personal fulfillment in their work. Most importantly, they discover that purpose isn't just an ideal—it's a practical force multiplier that drives performance and meaning.

This sounds good in theory, but how does it work in practice?

How do you focus on purpose when you're drowning in daily demands?

What differentiates leaders who merely survive from those who truly thrive?

We'll answer these questions in this book, drawing from established research and decades of experience working with hundreds of industry leaders who have successfully navigated these same challenges. We've had ringside seats to glorious successes and unfortunate failures, allowing us to identify patterns that separate those who merely survive from those who genuinely thrive.

One common challenge, whether you are new to your company or role or simply looking to level up in your current role, is figuring out how to be successful. Unfortunately, that is easier said than done. Research confirms that more than half of all executive transitions are unsuccessful.[1] These failures not only come at an enormous personal cost, but they typically cost the organization even more—upwards of 10x the executive's salary.[2]

The good news is that you can beat these odds and confidently step into your role. This starts by recognizing that succumbing to the tyranny of the urgent often prevents leaders from prioritizing what matters. The constant pressure of deadlines, stakeholder demands, and daily crises can consume your attention and zap your energy. However, exceptional leaders understand that long-term success requires looking beyond these immediate pressures.

What matters is doing the right things, the right way. This means delivering results in a manner that builds sustainable success and maintains integrity. It means resisting the temptation to take shortcuts or compromise values in pursuit of quick wins. For us, and we hope for you, this points to something much deeper, something we describe as *purpose-driven leadership.*

We intentionally choose these words to describe our approach because each represents a critical aspect of what we believe helps individuals and organizations thrive.

Driven leaders focus on delivering extraordinary results, ensuring that everything they do drives the organization's key performance indicators— sales, stock price, throughput, retention, profitability, customer satisfaction, or return on investment. They are unsatisfied with slightly better performance than last year; they are looking for ways to level up, ascend to new heights, and outperform even the most optimistic targets. They constantly tweak their priorities and plans to deliver jaw-dropping performance.

And yet, it's tempting to jump in and execute so fast that you lose track of what truly matters most, which are the most value-added tasks, and how to organize yourself and your team so that you can deliver on them. You can become so busy doing that you lose yourself in the process and unintentionally sabotage your efforts and your teams.

This is where successful leaders differentiate themselves.

Driven leaders narrowly focus on what matters most and don't mistake busyness for progress. Being frenetic, responding to the latest fire drill, delivering that next big initiative, and landing or saving that big "strategic" customer without being intentional about the process is a recipe for exhaustion and disappointment. Rather than succumbing to the tyranny of the urgent, they take a more measured approach. They understand that effectiveness comes not from constant motion but from purposeful action.

Purpose-driven leaders take it to the next level. They do not compromise their drive or commitment in deference to their values. Instead, they find ways to lean into doing what is right to achieve excellence. They are not merely leaders who are friendly (or less cut-throat). They operate in ways consistent with their values and embed those principles into everything they do. They also focus on helping those around them be their best, flourish, and help their organizations thrive. Purpose-driven leaders do the same things other leaders do, but differently, beginning with their mindset.

Over the years, we have led teams and organizations and coached hundreds of other leaders. We have had the privilege of ringside seats at some glorious successes and unfortunate failures. Many of the mistakes were preventable. We hope that by capturing them here, we can help you avoid them. More importantly, many of their successes are repeatable based on best practices. By studying and unpacking what factors drive these successes, you can build upon those principles and practices to achieve extraordinary success.

In observing these leadership journeys, we assert that it is possible to implement these best practices at any time. But, one of the most impactful times to do so is as you step into leading a new team, division, or organization. If you are stepping into a new senior leadership role, you are picking up this book at precisely the right time. If you are not, we encourage you to look at this as an opportunity to start afresh with some new or modified approaches to your existing role.

Either way, we hope that the principles here will be useful for you as you transform your leadership and, through it, your organization. These practical tips help you settle into your leadership groove, gain buy-in, establish credibility, and drive performance that delivers results–all without compromising your values.

To support you on this journey, we've designed this book to be practical and transformative. Rather than offering simple prescriptions or one-size-fits-all solutions, we provide frameworks, tools, and insights that you can adapt to your unique context and challenges. Whether you're taking on a new role or seeking to transform your current one, this book will help you confidently navigate the path to purpose-driven leadership.

How to Use This Book

While you can read it cover to cover, we've structured it as a strategic guide and a practical reference. We hope you find it a handy resource as you navigate and tackle the challenges ahead.

Just as every leadership journey has key milestones and critical decision points, we've organized this book to guide you through the essential elements of purpose-driven leadership in a clear, systematic way. Each part builds upon the previous ones, creating a roadmap for your transformation.

The Journey Ahead

This book is organized into three parts, each building on the foundation laid by the previous.

Clarify your focus	Invest in your capabilities	Deliver results
Connect with your purpose	Deepen purpose connection	Be an executive first
Asses the landscape	Upgrade your team	Lead with intention
Craft your vision	Tend to your culture	Architect your role
	Optimize ways of working	Practice agility

Part I: Get Clear on What Matters Most

The first three chapters help you establish the foundation for your success. You'll clarify your purpose, understand your landscape, and craft your vision. Whether you're in your first 90 days or looking to reset your leadership approach, this section is critical. We recommend spending quality time with these chapters before moving forward, as they create the bedrock for everything that follows.

Part II: Make Investments that Drive Success

The four chapters in the second section focus on building a framework for sustainable success. Here, you'll learn how to strengthen your team's connection to purpose, upgrade talent, build community, and optimize operations. These chapters focus on the architectural elements needed to support a high-performing organization.

Part III: Deliver Results

The final chapters discuss how to go from ideas to action. You'll learn how to architect your role, lead your team with intention, and ensure long-term success. This section helps you bring everything together to deliver extraordinary results.

Make the Most of This Resource

Each chapter includes practical frameworks, real-world examples, reflection questions, action items, and common pitfalls to avoid. The reflection questions will deepen your understanding by encouraging thoughtful analysis and action planning. They prompt you to capture specific examples, making insights more tangible and relevant to your experience.

By considering both the current state and the desired future state, you can identify gaps and opportunities for growth. The questions also help you pinpoint concrete actions, ensuring that reflection leads to meaningful progress. Setting timeframes for implementation adds accountability and structure, transforming insights into achievable steps toward improvement.

We recommend:

1. Reading each chapter's key takeaways first to grasp the main concepts

2. Working through the reflection questions to personalize the content
3. Completing key action items to put ideas into practice
4. Revisiting chapters as new challenges arise in your role

Additional Resources

We understand that while it's often easy to grasp a new concept, figuring out how to put it into practice can be much more challenging. To support you in applying the ideas we discuss, we've provided a variety of resources—such as assessment tools, planning templates, team exercises, and implementation guides. Rather than include all the details of these tools in the main text—which could make the book harder to read—we've chosen to reference them throughout and provide access in the Appendix and on our website (adlucemgroup.com).

Your Leadership Journey

Remember, becoming a purpose-driven leader is not a destination but a journey. While the first 90-100 days in a new role are particularly critical, the principles and practices in this book will serve you throughout your leadership career. Use this book as your guide, returning to relevant sections as you face new challenges and opportunities.

As you progress through the chapters, you'll notice that each builds upon the previous ones, creating an integrated approach to purpose-driven leadership. The concepts work together synergistically—the stronger your foundation (Part I), the more effective your investments (Part II) will be in driving results (Part III). But at the root of it all is your purpose and how it grounds and guides your leadership journey.

Key Chapter Takeaways

- Most executive transitions fail to meet expectations - but you can beat these odds.
- Success requires doing the right things in the right way.
- Purpose-driven leaders find ways to achieve excellence while staying true to their values.

Introduction Chapter Reflection Questions

1. What does purpose-driven leadership mean to you personally?
2. How do your values currently show up in your leadership approach?
3. What most excites you about the leadership opportunity ahead of you?
4. What fears or concerns do you have about your leadership transition?
5. Where might you need to adjust your mindset to succeed in your new role?

PART I

Get Clear on What Matters Most

Chapter 1

Connect With Your Purpose

Clarify your focus	Invest in your capabilities	Deliver results
Connect with your purpose	Deepen purpose connection	Be an executive first
Asses the landscape	Upgrade your team	Lead with intention
Craft your vision	Tend to your culture	Architect your role
	Optimize ways of working	Practice agility

"An extraordinary business starts with extraordinary people. Extraordinary people start with purpose." —Jesper Lowgren

Purpose is more than a buzzword or a feel-good concept—it's the fundamental force that drives extraordinary performance. It transforms mundane tasks into meaningful work, individual effort into collective achievement, and everyday leaders into catalysts for lasting change.

When organizations tap into authentic purpose, the results are remarkable. Teams become more innovative, employees more engaged, and outcomes more successful. But perhaps most importantly, purpose provides the resilience and clarity needed to navigate today's complex business environment.

Consider what prompts a call center agent to spend extra time on the phone with a customer whose spouse is deployed, a flight attendant to race through the airport to reconnect a passenger with their phone, or a teacher to spend their evenings developing innovative lesson plans.

USAA, Southwest Airlines, and City Year say it is their employees' passion for their purpose. That deep connection to why they exist drives their hard work and perseverance, pulling them through the drudgery and inspiring them to overcome obstacles. While it may not seem critical, it greatly impacts the bottom line. Organizations that tap into their purpose are significantly more innovative, successful, and profitable than others.[3] [4] [5]

Our sense of purpose drives us to engage and become the best version of ourselves. Purpose gives work more meaning. It shapes our mission and values and provides a North Star for our work, the clients we serve, the business model we develop, and the lives we are fortunate to live.

Shawn Askinosie's journey from a successful criminal defense lawyer to a purpose-driven chocolate maker exemplifies this transformative power of purpose. After experiencing burnout in law, he sought to establish a more meaningful work focus. He founded Askinosie Chocolate to serve farmers, customers, and the community - sharing profits directly with cocoa farmers, providing transparency in sourcing, and launching programs to feed thousands of students in Tanzania and the Philippines. Their Direct Trade profit-sharing model paid farmers significantly above market rates while building a globally recognized premium chocolate brand.[6] His company's success demonstrates how purpose-driven leadership can simultaneously deliver social impact and business results.

Purpose drives passion and can fuel transformation.[7] But it does more than that—it creates a legacy. The impact of purpose-driven leadership ripples far beyond immediate results, shaping both individual careers and organizational futures. When leaders ground their decisions in their purpose, they don't just achieve goals—they build lasting positive change that continues long after moving on.

Set the Foundation for Your Leadership Legacy

Your leadership journey isn't just about today's results - it's about the lasting impact you want to create. Research shows that leaders who consciously craft their legacy create more sustainable organizational value.[8] Those impacts manifest along three critical dimensions:

- People Impact: Developing others by connecting them to shared purpose and meaning
  - How have you developed others?
  - What capabilities have you built in your team?
  - Who will carry forward your values and approach?
- Organizational Impact: Building systems and culture that sustain purpose-driven success
  - What systems and processes will outlast your tenure?
  - How have you strengthened the culture?
  - What innovations have you enabled?
- Personal Impact: Creating transformative change that shapes your leadership legacy
  - What will you be remembered for?
  - How have you grown and evolved?
  - What wisdom will you pass on?

The transformative power of purpose isn't just theoretical–it's been demonstrated repeatedly in organizations of all sizes. Researchers Robert Quinn and Anjan Thakor[9] share a particularly impactful story about how DTE Energy, a large diversified energy company, underwent a metamorphosis by creating greater alignment between its purpose and daily tasks.

Employee engagement and profitability challenges at DTE that existed before 2007 were exacerbated by the Great Recession of 2008. Struggling to turn the situation around, DTE President Gerry Anderson took a fortuitous trip that unlocked a new way of thinking. At the invitation of Joe Robles, a DTE board member and CEO of USAA, Anderson visited the USAA headquarters in San Antonio, Texas.

Once there, his eyes were opened to the deep connection between USAA's employees and its mission and values. The connection was palpable. Their purpose was not just up on the walls; it was used to start every meeting and was at the forefront of each employee's mind as they went through their daily tasks. It guided nearly every activity in the company, beginning with recruiting. It was nurtured during onboarding, through intense cultural immersion and carefully curated orientation experiences, and maintained in the workforce via a deeply shared passion for serving those who serve.

USAA Mission Statement [10]

The mission of the association is to facilitate the financial security of its members, associates, and their families through provision of a full range of highly competitive financial products and services; in so doing, USAA seeks to be the provider of choice for the military community.

USAA Core Values

USAA's core values of Service, Loyalty, Honesty, and Integrity are the foundation upon which the association's heritage is based, and upon which its future depends. Each and every USAA employee is expected to embody these core values.

USAA Signature

We Know What It Means To Serve has long been USAA's signature. Every day, USAA's employees come to work for one reason, to serve members. Our signature is a reminder that we know what it means to serve like no one else.[11]

USAA's deeply embedded commitment to their purpose created undeniable results that inspired Anderson to rethink how they led at DTE. Anderson launched a series of transformational events culminating in the company's leaders crafting and dedicating themselves to DTE's purpose: "We serve with our energy, the lifeblood of communities and the engine of progress." As the changes took hold, engagement scores climbed, the company received a Gallup Great Workplace Award five years in a row, and financial performance followed suit, with DTE's stock price more than tripling in the period from 2008 to 2017.[12]

Regardless of subsequent or prior performance at these businesses, there is no doubt that they understood the impact of aligning behind vision and values. The connection to purpose provided a deeper meaning that employees could rally behind. As many business executives, researchers, and investors have discovered. Strong purpose-meaning-performance linkages are powerful and lead to better results.[13]

Conversely, look at the extreme cases of WeWork and Enron. Once valued at $47 billion, WeWork experienced a spectacular downfall in

2019 when its IPO revealed massive losses and questionable business practices under founder Adam Neumann's leadership. Similarly, Enron, once America's seventh-largest company, collapsed in 2001 after it was discovered that leadership had orchestrated one of the largest accounting frauds in history, destroying billions in shareholder value and employee pensions.

While there was undoubtedly a degree of smoke and mirrors around the company cultures and business models, the lack of sound values and a clear guiding purpose ultimately led to disaster. Unfortunately, the landscape is littered with numerous examples of corporate collapse due to greed, fraud, or misguided pursuits.

One unifying thread among leaders at these failed organizations is that they bought into the false dichotomy between purpose and profit.[14] They believed that by leaning into one, you were giving up on the other. However, research has established that this is not the case. The best and most successful organizations adopt a both-and approach. They know that a purpose-driven organization, well established in a firm set of clear values, will ultimately chart a more sustainable path to profit.[15]

Translating Organizational Purpose to Personal Leadership

While USAA and DTE Energy demonstrate the transformative power of purpose at an organizational level, purpose-driven leaders must have their connection to purpose. Just as these organizations create systematic approaches to embedding purpose throughout their operations, you'll need a structured approach to discovering and articulating your leadership purpose.

The first step is to understand your own "why." Consider what drives you. Look beyond achieving results.

What impact do you want to have?

What legacy do you want to leave?

Your answers to these questions will shape how you show up as a leader and influence how effectively you can inspire others.

Having a clear guiding purpose focuses your actions and decisions. It has been well established as a fundamental human motivator,[16] pulling us through the many challenges we will inevitably face. It becomes a force that motivates, inspires, and guides us, our teams, and our organizations. Furthermore, it drives higher levels of performance, individually and organizationally. Paradoxically, by focusing less directly on performance and centering on purpose, performance tends to be fueled as an inherent byproduct.

Yet, so many of us move through a frenzy of activity without stopping to center ourselves or those we lead on the North Star of our purpose. It's no wonder many executives report feeling overwhelmed as they attempt to guide and inspire their teams.

Before diving into specific exercises and frameworks, take a moment to reflect on what uniquely positions you to lead with purpose.

What experiences have shaped your leadership journey?

What values guide your decisions?

These reflections will help ground your purpose discovery process in authentic personal insight.

Align Personal and Organizational Values

Darius Mirshaahzadeh, in his book *The Core Value Equation: A Framework to Drive Results, Create Limitless Scale and Win the War for Talent,*[17] recounts his experience in a room full of sixty CEO's. When asked to show by standing how many of them had core values, the entire room of sixty stood. When asked to remain standing if they knew their core values off the top of their heads, thirty of them, a whole half of the room, sat down.

When asked to remain standing, if their *employees* knew their core values, 15 more sat down. Only two remained standing in this final group when asked how many could affirm that their *customers* knew their core values. Our experience across many organizations suggests that it would be an even worse result for a random sampling of employees and leaders.

Consider how Food Export, a nonprofit trade association focused on helping U.S. companies build their export business, approached this alignment challenge. Under the leadership of Executive Director/CEO Brendan Wilson, the organization recognized that it needed to refresh its organizational purpose and values to better guide its future direction. Rather than simply declaring new values from the top down, it engaged in a collaborative process that involved its entire team. This allowed it to clarify not just what it did but why it mattered and how everyone would work together.

The transformation process helped Food Export develop mission, vision, and values statements that were more than just words on a wall. They served as practical guideposts for decision-making and daily operations. These statements now function as a beacon for the organization, driving their commitment to peak performance and helping propel their nonprofit to new heights. Most importantly, because the process included the whole team, these guiding principles reflect authentic organizational values that resonate across all levels.

This example illustrates how organizations can transform abstract values into practical guardrails that guide decision-making and behavior.

Your values articulate who you are as an organization and what is most important. While organizational values provide guardrails for collective action, your leadership values must align with and amplify these broader principles. It strengthens your collective focus and helps everyone understand the organization. If your team or company values are empty platitudes or not tied to who you are, you will float rudderless, tossed about by the whim of every undercurrent you encounter. On the other hand, if you are in tune with what you stand for and what you are here to accomplish or deliver, you can navigate even the choppiest of waters as you set sail for your destination.

Take a few moments to write down your core values (the exercise is in Appendix 1A). As a leader, you'll want to consider your values (see Appendices 1A and 1B) and how they align with your organization's values (see Appendix 1C). This may also be an opportunity to augment or evaluate those already in place. If they do not yet exist in writing, it is worth taking the time to create them, capturing the essence of the organization. They should articulate the values you exhibit when you and your team are at your absolute best.

Once you've clarified your values, the next step is ensuring they accurately represent who you are. They should genuinely and authentically describe and embody who you are. This is critical for gaining the buy-in of both employees and customers.

Get Clear on Your Purpose

Your purpose is understanding and communicating what you deliver and why you exist. As we shared earlier, organizations and teams that know their purpose consistently outperform those who do not.

So, if the values above help you know yourself and your team, your purpose will help you understand your customers, your employees, and your role in delivering what they need. Alignment on that purpose will ultimately keep you on course through the rough seas of our volatile, uncertain, complex, and ambiguous world.[18]

Clarity of purpose provides you and your team with an unambiguous compass and roadmap for the journey, enabling you to make practical tradeoffs and decisions while staying aligned with one another and your ultimate goals.[19] They also drive performance, with a significant body of research supporting the purpose-performance connection across multiple industries and geographies.[20] There is a strong connection between stock value, profit, ROI, and strength of employee connection to purpose and values.[21]

To achieve this, your values and purpose must be inspirational, meaningful, and grounded in who you are at your very best. Your values should be clear, affirmative, authentic, and sticky. Affirmative and aspirational goals give everyone something to strive for, which is more motivational than a list of rules filled with "thou shalt nots." Stickiness is about making them catchy. It makes it easy for them to identify and remember up, down, and across the organization. It also makes them memorable for your customers.

Given these significant benefits, we encourage you to review your purpose statement if you have one or create it if you do not. This statement serves as a practical guide to harness and communicate your "big why" - what you are here for.[22] Explore where your purpose statement intersects with your values. Your purpose should also support the company's purpose. This raison d'etre (reason for being) establishes and communicates how you and your team will stay connected to deliver meaningful value to your organization and, ultimately, your customers.

If you do not have values and a purpose already articulated for your organization, we encourage you to consider creating them. You can use the framework provided in Appendix 1C. Then pressure test them with the following questions:

- Do they clearly answer the question, what do you want to be known for?
- Are they articulated in the affirmative (i.e., they do not contain "shall not" statements)?
- Are these your highest priority values (recommend not more than 5)?
- Do they genuinely reflect who you are or can reasonably be (it's okay to be aspirational, but they shouldn't be detached from reality)?
- Are they sticky? Do they have a short, engaging, memorable phrase of not more than a few words for each?

Before diving into specific frameworks and exercises, let's explore how to uncover and articulate your authentic purpose in a way that resonates personally and organizationally. This discovery process will help you align your aspirations with your organizational impact.

Establish Your Purpose Framework

Purpose reflection requires considering three key elements that intersect to reveal your authentic purpose:

- What you're great at (your talents and capabilities)
- What you're passionate about (what energizes and excites you)
- What creates value (what the world needs and will reward)

Your purpose lies at the intersection of these three elements. To help uncover it, consider:

1. Your origin story - what brought you to this point?
2. Your proudest achievements - what truly matters to you?
3. Your impact on others - how you create value?
4. Your sources of energy - what activities energize you?
5. Your legacy - what do you want to be remembered for?

See Appendix 1B for personal purpose discovery exercises and Appendix 1C for organizational purpose exercises to help you with this process.

Build Purpose-Driven Legacy

Creating a sustainable legacy requires an intentional focus on succession and systems.[23] The most enduring legacies come from leaders who build organizations that can thrive without them.[24] Consider Anne Mulcahy, who led Xerox's transformation from near-bankruptcy to sustainable success. Her legacy wasn't just a financial turnaround - she built leadership capabilities throughout the organization, strengthened the culture, and developed her successor from within.[25] [26] Years after her departure, the systems and values she established continued to guide the company.

Or take Ed Catmull at Pixar, who created not just a successful studio but a sustainable creative culture that consistently produces excellence.[27] His focus on building systems that support creativity and innovation, rather than depending on individual genius, enabled the studio to maintain its standards even after his retirement.

These leaders succeeded not by trying to do everything themselves but by creating conditions where others could excel. They understood that sustainable success is built on strategic planning, leadership development, and continuous growth. Strong succession plans ensure leadership continuity while documenting key learnings and approaches to preserve institutional knowledge for future success.

Developing future leaders fosters resilience and adaptability, providing a steady pipeline of capable decision-makers. Establishing enduring systems creates stability, while embedding purpose in processes aligns daily operations with long-term vision. Maintaining personal renewal and growth keeps leaders engaged and effective, preventing burnout. Balancing short-term results with long-term impact ensures lasting progress and meaningful contributions.

When leaders align their purpose with their leadership legacy aspirations, they create a powerful foundation for sustainable impact. Your purpose serves as the compass that guides daily decisions, while your legacy vision ensures these decisions build toward lasting positive change. This connection between purpose and legacy transforms not just your leadership approach but the very fabric of your organization.

Once you have clarity on what you and your team/organization are about, the next step is to clarify how you will add value. You must focus on leaning into it as a team. It should be the yardstick against which you will measure yourself and how you and your team connect to meaning at work.[28] It will also provide the foundation for your vision - a topic we will cover more deeply in Chapter 3. With your purpose distinctively defined, it is time to understand the landscape in which you will bring it to life. Even the most substantial purpose must fit well within the broader context to be effectively implemented.

Key Chapter Takeaways

- Values must be clear, affirmative, authentic, and memorable.
- Successful organizations and teams have deep connections to and are constantly inspired by their purpose and values.
- If you want to reach peak performance, the time you spend identifying, articulating, and/or optimizing your values and purpose statement is well spent.
- Successful leaders ensure that they and their teams maintain alignment with the organization's values and purpose.
- Purpose-driven leaders create a lasting impact by consciously crafting their legacy through developing others, building sustainable systems, and driving meaningful transformation.
- The most enduring legacies come from leaders who create conditions where others excel rather than trying to do everything themselves.

Chapter 1 Reflection Questions

1. What drives you to lead beyond just achieving results?
2. When have you felt most aligned with your purpose at work?
3. What are your non-negotiable values as a leader?
4. How well do your values align with your organization's stated values?

Chapter 2

Listen and Learn to Assess the Landscape

Clarify your focus	Invest in your capabilities	Deliver results
Connect with your purpose	Deepen purpose connection	Be an executive first
Asses the landscape	Upgrade your team	Lead with intention
Craft your vision	Tend to your culture	Architect your role
	Optimize ways of working	Practice agility

*"Of all the skills of leadership, listening is the most valuable —
and one of the least understood. Most captains of industry
listen only sometimes, and they remain ordinary leaders. But a
few, the great ones, never stop listening."*
—Peter Nulty, Fortune Magazine

"It's dishonorable to stay stupider than you need to be"
—Charlie Munger

At its core, effective leadership is about guiding yourself, your teams, and your organization in the right direction by choosing the optimal set of activities.[29] [30] But determining where best to focus requires you to learn about the situation you are stepping into.[31] [32] [33] [34] One temptation that many executives fall into when they take on new roles is to over-index on sharing their point of view in their passion for proving themselves. In their hurry to deliver, they rush to form opinions and plans.[35] [36] [37]

This approach is foolhardy and sets you up for failure. It signals to your new colleagues that you believe you know everything and expect them to fall in line. You demonstrate that you aren't willing to learn from others' expertise and experience. All of these are things that could have been avoided through thoughtful inquiry and observation.[38] As a purpose-driven leader, this closed mindset is the worst possible starting point - it fundamentally undermines both your credibility and your ability to lead effectively.[39] [40]

Listen First

We would like to begin by sharing the impact made when one of our colleagues resisted the urge to jump straight to action when stepping into the CEO role. Laura was appointed CEO as the former COO when past transgressions and unethical actions came to light. In this new role, she not only had to lead the company but also unearth the root causes of the unhealthy environment, drastically transform the culture, and help the company heal from the damage that had been caused.

It is challenging enough to step in and take the helm of a large organization, but doing so amidst a crisis that threatened to destroy the company from the inside out was practically impossible. The scandal had eroded trust at the executive level and in every part of the organization. It wasn't clear how she should handle the challenge ahead of her, and there certainly wasn't a playbook.

Laura would later share that the sheer scope and severity of the situation, and the lack of a clearly defined playbook, actually turned out to be a forcing mechanism, requiring her to understand and learn first. She scheduled listening tours across the organization with large cross-sectional groups. She opened them all by sharing that her intent was simply to listen and understand. She acknowledged that there were deeply rooted problems and the desire to understand as much as possible before developing a plan to address them.

She asked questions but mostly listened, allowing people to share their experiences, opinions, and perspectives. She shared her commitment to improving the organization and dedicated herself to that role. She ended every session by letting them know she would continue to listen and take appropriate action when she understood the situation well enough.

True to her word, Laura spent much of her first month as CEO actively listening and seeking to understand. However, once she thoroughly understood the situation, she shared her observations with her Board of Directors, used those insights to create a plan of action, and began executing her transformation strategy. A key part of her approach was maintaining transparency and rebuilding trust by communicating her plans to the entire organization. She transparently shared her observations, plans, and progress at regular town halls. And she always fielded questions.

Her ultimate success as a leader resulted not just from taking action but by gathering information and input. In this way, she developed a deep understanding of the situation, allowing her to tackle the challenges they faced from a more informed point of view. Once her listening tour was complete, she went on a sharing tour, reflecting on what she had learned and how it shaped her plans. She developed a reputation for transparency, leadership, and integrity.

Don't Let the Pressure to Deliver Make You Short-Sighted

Not all leaders are thrust into a situation that forces them to listen, but successful leaders prioritize seeking to understand before taking action. Attempting to demonstrate expertise before developing understanding inevitably backfires. Go on a listening tour first - it's the foundation for building credibility and trust with your new team.

When our client accepted a new position as the Chief Product and Technology Officer at a large multinational software and services company, she had a choice. Having done her due diligence before accepting the position and being a very experienced product and technology leader, she could easily have assumed she had enough information to develop her action plan and move into execution mode immediately.

In fact, given the pressure the CEO and Board of Directors were putting on her to deliver results quickly, most leaders might have crafted a plan that they could begin executing on day one. After all, the clock was ticking, budgets were already being finalized, and the board wanted an update within the quarter.

The months-long recruiting process allowed her to discuss extensive matters with nearly all the company's leaders. It also gave her enough time to vet everything she was hearing from external sources. Thus, she could have assumed she already knew everything she needed.

But she wisely resisted the temptation to assume she knew everything necessary and instead planned her listening tour. She even got help from us to conduct detailed interviews, knowing that it would both speed up and deepen the insights she would have at her disposal. We helped her avoid missing what MIT scholars have termed the "stealth mandate"[41] the expectations that are not immediately obvious but real nonetheless.

The systematic approach both of these leaders took to listening and learning provides a practical template for any executive transition. A wise leader prioritizes a sufficient understanding of the context before taking action. The trick, however, is not to delay action too long but to ensure you quickly gain enough information to make wise and decisive decisions. This requires a thoughtful approach to identifying stakeholders, asking questions, collecting data, and synthesizing findings.

When planning your listening tour, consider the perspectives you need carefully. Be sure to include stakeholders from across the organization and at all levels. In addition, look outside the organization, including customers, partners, vendors, industry experts, and even competitors. Start by exploring what's working well, where people see opportunities, and what they're most proud of. Then, dive deeper into specific areas for growth and innovation. You will find a detailed list of suggested questions and topics in Appendix 2A. Focus on understanding four key dimensions: external strategic opportunities, internal performance opportunities, operational capabilities, and personal/team dynamics.

All too often, strategic analysis is undertaken with a clinical lens and devolves into a rote exercise that both takes too long and results in a summary of what everyone already knows.[42] [43] Identifying strategic opportunities is all about possibility thinking. This requires embracing divergent thinking - generating multiple creative possibilities without judgment - and convergent thinking - analyzing and evaluating options to identify optimal solutions. While our natural tendency is to quickly converge on solutions, deliberately staying in a divergent mindset allows us to explore novel opportunities and challenge assumptions before narrowing our focus. It is about answering the key question, "What role would we play when we are our best selves in the market?"

Our colleague, Amber Johnson, advocates the power of asking great questions and suggests that the quality of the answers you receive is almost always related to the quality of the questions. Remember the adage, "Ask a stupid question, get a stupid answer?" Amber might reframe that to "ask a superficial question and get a superficial answer." If you want to go deep and get insightful, ask appropriate, open-ended questions, look for the correct data, and probe and listen for the responses you get.

Listen Authentically

Sometimes, when we are overwhelmed by new people, projects, goals, and expectations, we go through the motions without actively listening. Busyness and stress can be considerable barriers to overcome. Being aware of this tendency, you can remind yourself to listen for the most important ideas, information, strengths, and positive observations to celebrate and identify the challenges, goals, and processes that need to change. When your listening is authentic and active, it can have a powerful impact on performance.

One of our favorite research studies examined high, medium, and low-performing teams and studied their conversations. They found that members of high-performing teams typically spend only half their time advocating for their positions and ask as many questions of one another to better understand other team members' points of view, in balance with the number of times they advocate for their own positions.[44]

In other words, by listening to each other, asking questions, showing curiosity, and genuinely considering the ideas of others, we create the conditions for high performance. Most importantly, we must pay attention to the whole story and person because people want to be seen, heard, and appreciated. This takes real time, energy, and openness. However, the return on this investment is enormous regarding short— and long-term performance.

Listen to Data and Avoid Confirmation Bias

Learning about the organization should also include listening to internal and external data. These should contain the same types of information you ask for if you conduct due diligence during an acquisition. After all, you are effectively acquiring this business as a massive part of your personal portfolio and will invest most of your waking hours into building it.

As you wouldn't purchase a company without thorough due diligence and expert guidance, stepping into an executive role deserves the same rigorous analysis. Many leaders find that partnering with experienced advisors during this process accelerates their understanding, helps identify blind spots, and provides an objective perspective on the data. Like a skilled investment advisor helping evaluate an acquisition target, the right consulting/advisory partner can help you interpret the signals in the data and ask the questions you might not think to ask.

While the prospective list of documents you should ask for is long, generally, you will want to prioritize strategic and planning documents, financial and operational performance data, and data regarding the people, processes, technology, and systems that are core to your part of the business. In addition, you will want market and competitive data - data on competitors, suppliers, vendors, and customers. Be sure also to gather appropriate benchmark data, such as employee and customer surveys (including external data such as Glassdoor). This is the starting point for your assessment of the strategic landscape - it is your map of the world upon which you will build your strategy and vision, so you will want to be sure it is good. We have included a suggested due diligence checklist in Appendix 2B.

Lean into the data and look for surprises rather than merely confirmation of your pre-existing opinions. If the data shows you something you already know, ask yourself what that data might also indicate. For instance, a stable and relatively evenly distributed market share may confirm you are holding your own in the market, or it may indicate that others are equally well-positioned to take by stepping up their innovation efforts.

Additionally, looking at the external situation at a high level may mask underlying shifts. Two competitors may hold the same relative market share they always have. Still, when you do a deeper analysis, you may find they are focusing on separate subsegments that will ultimately make it easier for them to serve those segments better and increase the likelihood you won't be able to compete as well for either segment, putting your market position at significant risk.

Looking for what we expect to see can be an easy trap to fall into, one that scholars such as Kahneman[45] describe in great detail. If not actively fought against, confirmation bias can be our worst enemy. One of the most effective ways to combat that is to get other people to look at the situation and provide their perspective. So, while we recommend gathering your data, we even more emphatically recommend that you ask for the perspective of others on that data. To that end, we recommend scheduling and conducting a series of interviews with individuals both inside and outside the organization. Ask them how they see the situation, the opportunities and threats in the market, and what they might do if they could change anything.

We've provided a Strategic Relationship Tracker in Appendix 2D to help you systematically manage these important relationships over time. This practical tool will help you maintain meaningful connections and ensure that no crucial relationships fall through the cracks as you build and nurture your network.

Identify External Opportunities

One of our (and Warren Buffett's) favorite business success stories is Nebraska Furniture Mart (NFM),[46] having consistently outperformed both competitors and the stock market. NFM accomplished this by understanding what their customers needed and establishing a way to deliver it to them consistently. They understood what the customers wanted, where the current competitors failed to deliver, and how their capability set positioned them to meet those needs effectively. Their apparent strategy, strong business values, and effective leadership enabled them to develop the capabilities needed to be the low-cost furnishings provider in Omaha and beyond. When developing the plan for her business, founder and matriarch Rose Blumkin (Mrs. B) established a strategy that NFM was uniquely positioned to deliver - affordable, high-quality household furnishings.

Mrs. B was a force of nature, having escaped from a small village and traveled across Russia and the Pacific Ocean as a teenager to emigrate to the US. In 1917, she landed in America without speaking a word of English.[47] She and her husband opened a used clothing store in Omaha in 1919, and in the hard times of the 1930s, Mrs. B set up a used furniture business in the basement that would become NFM. The purpose and operating model she held fast to was to "sell cheap and tell the truth." Despite her diminutive size, she became a competitive giant, often frustrating and infuriating the local retailers. This resulted in her being taken to court for "unfair business practices" for underpricing her competitors. Not only did the judge find in favor of Mrs. B, but he also purchased carpet from her!

From its beginnings over 80 years ago, NFM targeted a unique place in the market. They sold furnishings cheaper than other retailers in the area.[48] Having failed to pressure Mrs. B into raising her prices, her competitors banded together to get local furniture manufacturers to stop selling to her. Rather than being driven out of business or convinced to raise prices, Mrs. B purchased from manufacturers in other parts of the country and maintained her low-price policy.[49]

> *NFM has been guided by principles of selling cheap, telling the truth and providing outstanding selection and service. By keeping our principles in mind, we believe we can fulfill our true mission: Improving people's lifestyles. - NFM Vision* [50]

NFM carved out a place for itself as a store that provided selection and savings. Even when NFM had established itself as a dominant player in the market, and competition was low, they chose to forego the option to increase margins by raising prices Instead, they held fast to their values, purpose, and strategy, entrenching their reputation and cementing customer loyalty. They grew profits by increasing selection and expanding to new locations while sticking to their low-price promise that engendered loyalty and enabled customers to improve their lifestyles.

Warren Buffett famously shared, "I'd rather wrestle grizzlies than compete with Mrs. B and her progeny. They buy brilliantly, they operate at expense ratios competitors don't even dream about, and they then pass on to their customers much of the savings."[51] NFM stuck to its values and used them to guide its choices and seize market opportunities.

As you consider the external opportunities available to your organization, evaluate all the external factors that affect the business, but consider them within the context of your purpose. Build a fundamental analysis - get the data and develop some hypotheses. But let this be your starting point, not your finished product. This should be the working model upon which you flesh out your hypotheses; for that, you will need external perspectives. Some of the key areas to focus on include:

- **Market Reality:** Consider the market's current size, profit margins, cost structure, key success factors, and barriers to entry. Evaluate how these are trending and how they are forecasted to change.

- **Competitive Environment:** Consider the competitive structure of the industry, including the factors that contribute to the power of suppliers, vendors, competitors, buyers, and distributors. Porter's Five Forces framework provides a systematic approach to analyzing these competitive dynamics by examining the threat of new entrants, the bargaining power of suppliers, the bargaining power of buyers, the threat of substitute products or services, and rivalry among existing competitors.[52]

- **Industry Landscape:** Consider the current and potential future political, legal, regulatory, economic, technological, and social context and how it might affect the business. This can be unpacked with the PESTLE analysis (Political, Economic, Social, Technological, Legal, and Environmental factors). This framework helps analyze these external macro-environmental factors that can impact your organization's success.

Once you have a first pass at these elements, take a step back and look at them through the lens of your organization's purpose. If your organization were at its absolute best and seizing the opportunities available, how would it show up?

Would you be setting the standard for customer service?

Would you be the lowest-cost provider?

What aspects of the purpose would allow you to show up in a valuable and unique way?

Value-added innovation most often comes not from creating fundamentally new ideas but rather, new constructs built on concepts that are already known.

Schedule time internally with key leaders and individuals who have a deep understanding of the business, technology, and industry, with unique perspectives. What you are trying to create is a wide diversity of expert opinions that, when taken together, will enable you to craft a unique perspective on the business.

As we know from the extensive research done on creativity,[53] value-added innovation most often comes not from creating fundamentally new ideas but rather new constructs built on concepts that are already known. So much of the value you are likely to create comes down to understanding and combining what is already understood in a way that adds significant value to the business.[54]

Questions to consider:

- What is the organization's most significant strategic opportunity?
- Can you describe the company's biggest market challenge in one sentence?
- What do customers/partners/suppliers think about the company? Has that changed?
- What one thing (if we could change it) would significantly impact our future?
- What has this organization accomplished in recent years that is new and noteworthy? Have we communicated it widely and taken full advantage of it?

Assess Internal Capabilities

As you consider the organizational capabilities, evaluate the strengths and weaknesses of the organization and how they affect the value you add to the market. What unique strengths do you have relative to competitors, and what potential weaknesses do you need to overcome? When trying to determine this, start with the organization's purpose and the unique organizational characteristics connected to it.

Let us highlight an organization that has significantly impacted the coffee industry to illustrate the strong link between purpose and capabilities.

Sustainable Harvest sources and imports coffee from around the world. At the heart of its business is its mission to improve transparency and sustainability when sourcing coffee. Doing so helps ensure that farmers are paid fairly for their coffee beans and that coffee roasters can access sustainably grown, high-quality beans. They have made significant investments in relationships with growers worldwide to support this mission. They have helped growers build connections with roasters and other key stakeholders in the coffee supply chain.[55]

The capabilities supporting Sustainable Harvest's mission are distinctive and difficult to replicate. Their expertise in coffee growing and sourcing, combined with technology that enables tracking from farm to cup, creates unprecedented transparency in the coffee supply chain. Even more valuable are their deep relationships with growers across the globe. These partnerships allow them to influence the growing process, ensuring quality and sustainability in ways competitors struggle to match.

This focus on building unique capabilities mirrors NFM's success in the retail furnishing space. Just as Sustainable Harvest created a competitive advantage through deep supplier relationships and technical expertise, NFM built unmatched capabilities in sourcing high-quality goods at low prices while maintaining minimal overhead costs. In both cases, these organizations developed capabilities that aligned perfectly with their purpose while creating a sustainable competitive advantage.

While the best place to start assessing your internal capabilities is to ask how they support your purpose, you will also want to consider how these capabilities enable you to add value. Consider your organization's value delivery chain—from idea to customer purchase. Unpack how each value chain component contributes to its strengths or weaknesses in the marketplace.

For example, a high-speed, incredibly flexible production line might allow for rapid responses to shifts in market demand. A high-volume production line optimized for a single product might lower consumer costs. When evaluating each stage of your value delivery process, examine its strengths and weaknesses and how they collectively enhance your overall capabilities.

How has the company leveraged them in the past?

How will it affect the business's ability to compete as you consider the future?

Once you have a clear picture of your internal capabilities, you can collaborate with others–including trusted advisors, consultants, or mentors who can provide objective outside perspectives–to pressure-test your assumptions and expand your understanding. Their experience across multiple organizations and industries can help identify blind spots and opportunities you might otherwise miss.

Sample questions to consider for your discussions can be found in Appendix 2A.

Leverage Your Operational Resources

The resources you leverage to deliver value are connected to the organization's internal capabilities. Assessing the value-add of these tangible and intangible assets provides a resource-based view of the business.[56] [57] Tangible resources, such as financial and physical assets, can easily be understood from financial or accounting statements. For insurance companies like Geico, a strong balance sheet and healthy float (the margin between insurance premiums and insurance payouts) can create competitive strength.

Other businesses and industries may rely more on intangible assets such as brand, reputation, proprietary capabilities, or intellectual property. Coca-Cola's most significant assets are intangible - its world-renowned brand and its proprietary Coke recipe. By contrast, innovation capabilities are the most valuable intangible resources for Pixar, Apple, and Bell Labs. These resources are difficult to replicate and provide a sustainable strategic advantage when leveraged effectively.[58]

As you assess your resources, consider how you manage and use them. Are they consistent with your organization's purpose and values? For example, USAA's focus on "serving those who serve"[59] means that its staff must be able to relate to those in the military, understanding the challenges and situations they face.

To ensure this is the case, their recruitment strategy, training, onboarding programs, and customer service approach must support this. As a result, they actively hire veterans, military spouses, and those who are members of the National Guard and Reserve. Military acumen is a core component of their onboarding and training programs and is even highlighted in the exhibits and artwork on display in their San Antonio headquarters. Furthermore, they maintain a strong brand connection to the military, supported by investments in advertisements featuring military personnel and sponsorship of military-affiliated events such as the Army-Navy Football game.

As you consider your organization's operational resources, assess which impacts how you deliver your mission most.

What is the current status of these assets?

Which resources are you using well and effectively supporting, versus which seem to be floundering or not well leveraged?

How are your employees doing - what is working vs. what is not?

Once your thoughts and questions are captured, reach out to others for additional input to expand your perspective.

Questions to consider:

- What are our organization's core capabilities?
- What people, processes & technology are driving success?
- What strengths do I want to protect / not break (team, stakeholders)?
- What are our company resources – assets, intellectual property, and people?
- How are we using our resources well?
- How do our employees or shareholders perceive us?
- How are we meeting our employees' needs?

Create Your Purpose-Driven Assessment

Once you have completed your interviews and analyses, combine them into an overall assessment of what matters most to the organization.

While many leaders default to a traditional SWOT analysis, purpose-driven leaders need a framework that ensures strategic choices advance organizational purpose while building sustainable success. We recommend a structured approach that evaluates opportunities and challenges through five key lenses:

1. Purpose Alignment - How well do opportunities align with your organizational purpose and values?
2. Capability Assessment - What strengths can you leverage, and what capabilities must you build?

3. Impact Evaluation - How will your choices create sustainable value? How will they affect your various stakeholder groups?

4. Implementation Readiness - How prepared is your organization to execute effectively?

5. Action Planning - What specific steps will turn insight into impact?

This framework (detailed in Appendix 2C) helps you move beyond surface-level analysis to make strategic choices that serve your purpose while building lasting value. It provides a practical way to organize your insights while maintaining focus on what matters most.

Remember that assessment isn't a one-time exercise. Regular review and refinement of your understanding will help ensure your strategy remains relevant and actionable as circumstances change.

Once your assessment has come together, test it with others.

Last, and perhaps most important, pressure test it with others once your assessment has come together. Revisit some of the key individuals you interviewed and confirm you have put together the picture correctly and haven't missed anything.

Most importantly, ask, "Does this fit with your understanding of the situation?" If it doesn't, ask why. But if it does, ask why no one has done anything to address the challenges yet. You may get an insightful and critical answer to your success.

One leader we know stepped into a significant supply chain role and surfaced a major strategic disconnect during their onboarding. This leader probed why these known problems hadn't already been addressed. It became clear that several sacred cows, including the CEO's unwillingness to make specific changes, had shut down all prior efforts to address the situation. Clearly, this was not an ideal situation. Finding out early in his tenure enabled him to use his newness and mandate for change to get the backing and flexibility he needed to make changes that hadn't previously been possible.

Put Your Assessment into Practice

We know this sounds like a lot to take on before you ever get to the real work of your day job, but it is an investment well worth your time, as it will help ensure you are focusing on the right thing and have prioritized the most impactful actions.[60] As one colleague of ours memorably points out, you can spend <u>a little time</u> now focused on getting it right or <u>weeks and months</u> later trying to clean up all the mistakes and fallout. We know which we prefer.

We recognize that no assessment is ever finished, as your knowledge and the situation will continue to evolve. You will likely learn things in the coming weeks and months that will have you revisiting and refining your assessment. Despite that, incorporate what you have gleaned from this assessment and use it as your foundation as you enter your new role.

The next chapter will discuss clarifying your mandate and creating your vision. Your thorough assessment of the landscape has given you the context needed to clarify your mandate and craft a compelling vision. This is where your purpose meets reality and transforms into actionable direction.

Key Chapter Takeaways

- Resist the temptation to jump into action; take time to understand first.
- Begin by listening, researching, and learning, starting with a listening tour.
- Gather data from multiple internal and external sources as a due diligence exercise.
- Assess the external market from a variety of perspectives.
- Assess internal capabilities and how they contribute to strategic advantage.
- Summarize the situation and prioritize the opportunities, testing your hypotheses with others before finalizing.

Chapter 2 Reflection Questions

1. What are the most critical knowledge gaps you need to fill?
2. Who are the primary stakeholders you need to understand better?
3. What assumptions might you be making about the organization?
4. Where could you gather more diverse perspectives about the situation?

Chapter 3

Clarify Your Mandate and Craft Your Vision

Clarify your focus	Invest in your capabilities	Deliver results
Connect with your purpose	Deepen purpose connection	Be an executive first
Asses the landscape	Upgrade your team	Lead with intention
Craft your vision	Tend to your culture	Architect your role
	Optimize ways of working	Practice agility

"Leadership is the capacity to translate vision into reality."
—Warren Bennis

Now that you have a solid understanding of the landscape [Chapter 2] and are well-grounded in purpose [Chapter 1], it's time to translate those insights into a clear direction. While many leaders rush to action, purpose-driven leaders take time to ensure their mandate is clear and their vision compelling. This clarity guides your actions and enables you to align and inspire your team.

Consider Sarah, a newly appointed Chief Technology Officer at a global software company. Despite pressure from the board for quick results, she resisted the urge to launch initiatives based solely on her pre-hire discussions. Instead, she clarified her mandate with primary stakeholders, tested her understanding against the organizational landscape she'd assessed, and crafted a vision that would truly transform the organization. This thoughtful approach enabled her to deliver immediate improvements and build sustainable capabilities that continued driving value years later.

Our intent in this chapter is to lay out the best practices for crafting a vision that inspires the organization, focuses your efforts, and engages your team. We will discuss how to transform your initial mandate into a clear, actionable direction; align your vision across individual, team, and organizational levels; engage your team in co-creating the path forward; and create a practical transformation plan that delivers results.

However, leaders often stumble at this critical juncture, even with the best intentions. Let's examine the most common mistakes and how to avoid them.

Avoid common mistakes

The two most common and dangerous mistakes new leaders make are 1) acting too quickly, particularly before fully understanding the situation, and 2) taking on too much.

New leaders often have a limited understanding of the situational context they are stepping into, making it easy to miss potential problems. As a result, they feel "ready" to take action well before they actually are. Bill, a colleague of Melissa's and a very accomplished executive, made precisely this mistake early in his tenure at a large insurance company. When he was first hired, he received a clear mandate from his boss, took those as his marching orders, and moved out to begin making it happen. He assumed he had clarity, alignment, and his leader's full backing to accomplish it as quickly as possible. Several weeks into his tenure, he was making significant progress on his mandate, but was shocked when he was called on the carpet by none other than the boss, who had laid out his mandate and hand-selected him for the job.

The problem was that Bill walked in, thinking he knew everything he needed to know. He immediately began making changes, assuming he had the full authority to do so. As you can imagine, Bill stepped on landmines, which he was unaware existed. And, of course, his boss began receiving "feedback" from all over the company. Bill looks back on this with the clarity of experience and describes it as his first realization that the most important thing an executive must do is navigate complex realities and gain alignment with many different stakeholders. Your mandate is rarely as simple as it was presented when it was handed to you. The unarticulated expectation is that you will fully understand the organizational context, clarify and refine your mandate, and gain broad stakeholder alignment before laying out your vision and plan.

You will also need to consider mastering the political chessboard and organizational culture. Strong allies and good intelligence are essential to accomplishing the work ahead effectively. Rather than going into this in detail here, we will tackle it in Chapter 5.

Like Bill, it is incredibly easy to find yourself in a situation where you are surprised by missed expectations or realities you overlooked. This is precisely why you spent significant time unpacking the situation in the last chapter. Thanks to the detailed listening tour and the data you have gathered, you should clearly understand the opportunities (and challenges) you face. You likely also have a high-level sense of your priorities for the work ahead of you and your team. But resist the temptation to jump right in without appropriate forethought. You will be well served to consider how best to target your efforts carefully.

It's likely at this point that you've had a few surprises, come to understand things that have shifted both your focus and your priorities, and may be rethinking your action plan. That's a good thing. You have prevented the most common mistake leaders often make - being in such a hurry to demonstrate their value that they assume they know both the challenge ahead and the best course of action. Instead, you have taken the opportunity to learn, develop a plan, and act. It's "ready, aim, fire" for a reason.

The second mistake leaders make is tackling too much, believing that it must all be begun immediately, with so much to be done. But decades of data and research[61] [62] confirm Robert Browning's wisdom that "less is more"[63] plays out in nearly all operational contexts.[64] [65] This is never more true than when you are attempting to drive transformation. Focusing your efforts by launching a few highly impactful projects allows you to get them over the finish line, deliver impactful results, and move to the next. And it does the same for your team and your organization.

Furthermore, it enables you to maximize the productive time for yourself and your team rather than losing much of it to context switching. It can feel incredibly risky to start fewer things, almost as if you are limiting the upside potential. However, betting on fewer of the right things can make all the difference in the results you will see in the bottom line. [We discuss this further in Chapter 7.]

Now that you understand your situation more clearly, it's time to target your efforts and your team's. But take it step by step as you put together the best plan possible for tackling the challenge ahead.

Put Yourself in the Picture and Identify Your Teachable Point of View

First, take a step back from the situation and reground yourself. Consider what you bring to the organization. You were selected for this role for a reason, and you have something extraordinary to offer. Take a moment to sit back and reflect on your teachable point of view.[66] What unique perspective do you bring to this role that makes you the perfect candidate?

What combination of experience and inclination comes together to make you the ideal leader for this very moment?

What unique capabilities, strengths, and experiences do you have that would be valuable to bring to bear in this role?

We encourage you to reflect on and capture what makes you the perfect leader for this moment. Begin with a quick self-inventory using the 5x5 approach described below (and in Appendix 3A). In bodybuilding, the 5x5 technique is supposed to help you build strength, grow muscles, and break plateaus. Similarly, a leadership 5x5 enables you to unpack your strengths in ways that drive performance.

Here's how it works. Ask yourself the following five questions, capturing five answers for each.

What is unique about my:

1. **Capabilities**: What unrivaled capabilities do I possess?
2. **Knowledge**: What specialized knowledge do I hold?
3. **Experience**: What extraordinary experiences have I had?
4. **Perspective**: What novel perspective do I bring?

5. **Approach**: What specialized approaches to problem solving and work do I have?

Once you have this 5x5 list:

- **Identify the top 5 standouts** on this list that you believe make you extraordinary, particularly for this role.
- Then, **consider how those five things can be combined** and work together to create unparalleled leadership in this role.
- Now, **distill those into a single 2-3 sentence statement summary** of what you bring to bear in this role that will be the strength from which you lead.

This 2-3 sentence statement is your teachable point of view.

Clarify Your Mandate

Once you've established your teachable point of view, you have a clearer sense of the unique value you bring to this role. This self-awareness provides a foundation for the next critical step: clarifying your mandate in practical, actionable terms.

While your teachable point of view focuses on what you bring to the organization, your mandate defines what the organization needs from you. Aligning these elements creates powerful momentum for transformation. Your unique capabilities and perspective become the lens through which you interpret and execute your mandate, making your approach distinctive and effective.

Moving from self-understanding to organizational action, you'll often need to translate broad directives into specific, measurable objectives your team can rally behind. Many leaders stumble in this translation process by accepting vague mandates that lack clear success criteria or imposing their interpretation without sufficient stakeholder alignment.

While mandates often start broad, successful executives translate them into clear, actionable directives. To illustrate how this works in practice, consider these examples of how leaders might transform vague directives into specific, measurable mandates to drive meaningful change.

- **Example 1: Technology Transformation.** Consider a CTO who receives the initial mandate: "Modernize our technology infrastructure." This lacks the specificity needed to align stakeholders and drive action. Through conversations with the CEO, peers, and team, the mandate could be clarified to: "Create a cloud-first, scalable technology platform that reduces operating costs by 30% while enabling rapid product innovation and maintaining 99.99% reliability." This clarification provides clear direction (cloud-first architecture), measurable outcomes (30% cost reduction, reliability metrics), business impact (enable innovation), and stakeholder alignment (operations, product, finance)

- **Example 2: Sales Organization Rebuild.** In another scenario, a sales leader might face the directive to "fix the sales organization." Through stakeholder discussions, this could evolve into: "Build a consultative sales force that can double enterprise revenue in 3 years while maintaining 40% gross margins and reducing customer acquisition costs." This clarified mandate defines the approach (consultative selling), sets specific targets (revenue, margins), establishes a timeline (3 years), and connects to broader business goals.

- **Example 3: Cultural Transformation.** A Chief People Officer might be mandated to "improve company culture." Success requires more definition, and working with the leadership team could clarify this: "Create an innovative, high-performance culture that increases employee engagement scores from 65% to 85%, reduces turnover to under 10%, and delivers two major innovations annually. This clarification provides cultural characteristics (innovative, high-performance), specific metrics (engagement, turnover), performance expectations (innovation targets), and a clear measurement framework.

In each scenario, the key to transforming vague directives into clear mandates involves:

1. Engaging primary stakeholders to understand actual needs
2. Establishing specific, measurable outcomes
3. Connecting to broader business objectives
4. Creating clear accountability
5. Setting realistic timelines

Clarifying your mandate provides direction and builds alignment and support for your vision. It transforms abstract goals into concrete actions your team can rally behind and deliver.

Align Your Vision

With clarity about your mandate, it's time to ensure your vision aligns across individual, team, and organizational levels. This is crucial for creating and delivering meaningful transformation. Rather than creating a highly complex vision, we urge you to be as clear and concise as possible. Mrs. B's simple focus on "selling cheap, telling the truth, and providing outstanding selection and service" is a great example.[67] It is strategy at its finest. Your transformation plan cascades from this, allowing you to craft the path toward fulfilling your strategy.[68]

Start by revisiting the purpose work you completed in Chapter 1 (see Appendices 1B and 1C). Your vision should build on this foundation while addressing three critical questions:

- Individual Vision: How will you lead to create maximum impact?
- Team Vision: How will your team deliver unique value?
- Organizational Vision: How does this support the company's overall purpose and strategic goals?

Strong vision alignment can be tested by asking yourself a few questions:

- How do these visions support each other?
- Where might there be tensions to address?
- What adjustments would create better alignment?

You are on the right track if your answers are clear and show alignment. By contrast, if your vision emphasizes innovation but your team's vision focuses on operational excellence, you'll need to reconcile this potential conflict. Similarly, refinement is needed if your team vision doesn't clearly support and drive organizational purpose forward.

Vision alignment isn't about perfect matching—it's about creating a complementary focus that maximizes individual fulfillment and collective success.

Create a Transformation Story

Armed with your observations about the organization's opportunities, your teachable point of view, and your vision, you are now prepared to craft a transformation plan. Distill what you heard and use it to craft a transformation story you and your team can own.

Seize the opportunity to check with your leadership to confirm or refine your mandate. Your understanding of the organization's mandate may have also evolved. With this more informed picture of the situation, you will want to gain alignment on your mandate.

Because this transformation plan will need to be something your team can own and management can back, you will need to engage the wider group. Take the time to check back in with management and other stakeholders to confirm your new understanding of the mandate and ensure it aligns with theirs.

As you draft your transformation strategy, be sure your plan answers these fundamental questions:

- What does success look like for you and your team?
- How will you improve the business in your new role, and what areas require focus?
- What do you see as possible and achievable?
- What will you need to prioritize or de-prioritize?
- How will you contribute to the company's most significant strategic opportunity?
- And finally, how will you drive excellence, performance, and overall business progress?

By thoughtfully addressing these questions, you can develop an impactful strategy aligned with organizational goals.

Set your high-level strategy and transformation goals with clear targets for your first quarter. Begin by drafting what you believe they are and articulating what success would look like. The Appendix for Chapter 3 includes a template to help you with this.

This should include expectations for how you will not only transform the organization but simultaneously:

1. **Fulfill the requirements of your "day job":** By this, we mean fulfilling your team's contribution to delivering business as usual. In finance, this is closing the books every month. In sales, this means meeting target revenue goals. In manufacturing, this means meeting quality and production goals. Etc.

2. **Identify and deliver quick wins:** You do not have the luxury of waiting three months to demonstrate your value. Take the opportunity to build a reputation with short-term wins that matter to the company. When identifying potential quick wins, look for opportunities at the intersection of high impact and low complexity - initiatives that can be completed within 60-90 days, require minimal cross-functional dependencies, and deliver clear, measurable value aligned with your mandate. The best quick wins often address visible pain points that, when solved, build credibility with both your team and your stakeholders while creating momentum for more extensive transformational efforts.

3. **Develop appropriate systems:** Develop a system (put a process in place) that ensures you meet all your stated goals while

keeping you and your team at the top of your game. These are the set of actions and processes that automate keeping the trains on the tracks, enable your success, and ensure you continue to improve.

4. **Identify and plan for longer-term, bigger wins:** Put longer-term goals in place and undertake the tasks that will set you and your team up to deliver on these bigger goals, or big, hairy, audacious goals (BHAGs).[69]

These four focus areas provide the foundation for your transformation plan. See Appendix 3B for a detailed template and framework to help you develop each component.

Leverage Co-Creation

Now that you've established your perspective on what must be done, how do you ensure it becomes a reality? You must get widespread buy-in. Rather than being the sole author of this transformation plan, bring your team in and work together on your vision of the future and transformation story.

Ensure that while your fingerprints are all over it, your team feels like it's theirs, too. Walk that line well. Having your teachable point of view is important, but now you must balance that with the team's input as you build the path forward for the organization. This has to be something that everyone can get behind and be passionate about. Successful transformation stories are co-created with your team's active engagement.

Decisions are often made at the executive level, where the "folks on the ground" are left out of the process. The problem with this approach is that your broader team, including frontline workers, often have critical perspectives that are missed completely.[70] Suppose you can better harness your team's wisdom, energy, and commitment. In that case, this will better inform your strategic decisions and the likelihood of actually achieving them.[71] [72] [73] However, if you don't take time to make sure the appropriate people in your pit crew are aligned with your direction and approach, your car is not going to perform to its capabilities. When you allow your pit crew to participate in the process, you will come up with better solutions and stand a far better chance of winning your race.

When running a team, organization, department, or company, decisions must be made quickly. As a leader, it can often feel like you are building the car while driving it, and it is faster just to do it yourself. Yet, people support what they help to create. Purpose-driven leaders work with their teams and cultivate processes that support joint authorship and ownership. Rather than presenting fully-formed solutions, they engage their teams in shaping both the vision and the path forward.

People support what they help create.

Research from Harvard shows that when people are involved in creating something, they value it more highly and, as such, are more bought into it. While observed and documented in several contexts, there is a clear cognitive bias toward things individuals created themselves. Specifically, they tend to both place a higher value and greater loyalty on things they participated in creating. This phenomenon is called the *IKEA effect* because participants in one study assessed the value of the furniture they assembled to be higher than comparable or even higher quality furniture they did not put together. Furthermore, people support what they help to create. Given the benefits of this dynamic, it is incumbent upon leaders to harness this power and develop processes that support this co-creation.

One of our early clients was an electric grid management company. As one might imagine, the power industry is highly regulated and emphasizes cybersecurity. In its early days, a creative and energetic start-up spirit permeated the company's culture. As the company grew and regulatory requirements increased, the organizational landscape shifted from an agile and autonomous culture to a more controlled and bureaucratic environment.

In this new context, the company struggled to get out of its way and innovate. When they did try to innovate, their efforts were more "bolt-on" updates than real transformation. Employee engagement levels were not where they wanted them to be. There was a general malaise as employees felt uninspired and under-challenged. Consequently, the company struggled to hit its ambitious targets. To make matters worse, a large company in the region was poaching its top talent with promises of more engaging work, an exciting culture, and better compensation.

The company sought to stem the tide of disengagement and attrition, reinvigorate its workforce, and capture some of the entrepreneurial spirit and innovation that had fallen away in recent years. A new leader was appointed, and they realized they couldn't simply snap their fingers and wish this problem away. If they were going to turn the organization around, everyone needed to be part of crafting the solution.

They undertook a large-scale transformation summit that galvanized their efforts and refocused their 3-year strategic plan. During this process, they identified six key initiatives (a significantly smaller number than the laundry list of prior proposals) and received executive backing for their plan. Individuals could self-select into the project initiatives they were most passionate about.

When developing their plan in isolation, the newly appointed leader of this department had considered some but not all of these initiatives and had not structured them as well as the wider group did. When reflecting on the outcome, the leader observed that the co-created plan was better than any they would have crafted in isolation. Moreover, this approach engendered more ownership. It created an increased sense of unity, breaking down former silos and providing a shared vision around which employees could coalesce.

Employees reported being inspired by the process. One employee confessed that he had been actively pursuing employment outside the organization. However, this revitalizing event and process caused him to change his mind and look inside the organization for how/where he could best contribute his skills and passions. In the following months, engagement improved, and there was a more explicit focus on the strategic outcomes the organization sought to achieve.

Choose Your Co-Creation Approach

While the value of co-creation is clear, executing it requires structured approaches that engage stakeholders meaningfully.[74] Some proven approaches you may be familiar with are strategic summits, innovation workshops, and design sprints. While this is not an exhaustive list of examples, it samples some proven practical approaches in different situations. They should give you a sense of how to facilitate co-creation by embedding it into practices you may be familiar with.

1. **Strategic summits** bring together 50-100 stakeholders for intensive one—to two-day sessions that rapidly build alignment and create actionable plans. These large-scale meetings begin by sharing organizational context and data and then move to defining collective success criteria. Participants work together to generate potential solutions, build detailed implementation plans, and create broad ownership for the path forward.

2. **Innovation workshops** offer a more focused approach, bringing cross-functional teams together to tackle specific challenges. These smaller sessions challenge current assumptions and generate creative solutions. Teams prototype potential approaches, test concepts with stakeholders, and continuously refine them based on feedback.

3. **Design sprints** provide a structured way to prototype and refine solutions rapidly. These intensive sessions follow a clear progression: defining specific problems, creating potential solutions, testing approaches, gathering feedback, and iterating based on learning. This systematic approach helps teams move quickly from concept to tested solution.

Make Co-Creation Work in Practice

Once you've identified an appropriate co-creation approach, you will need to establish clear expectations and frameworks to execute it effectively.

First, set clear parameters for the process. Define the scope of what can and cannot be changed, establish who has the authority to make different types of decisions, and create clear timelines for the work. This clarity helps participants contribute meaningfully within established boundaries.

Second, ensure diverse participation throughout the process. Include people from different organizational levels, functions, and backgrounds. This diversity of perspective and experience leads to richer solutions and broader buy-in for the changes ahead.

Third, psychological safety should be created to enable authentic participation. Encourage open dialogue and welcome all ideas, even those that challenge current thinking. Focus on learning rather than judgment, and ensure people feel safe taking reasonable risks.

Fourth, action planning should be built into the process from the start. Move systematically from ideas to implementation by assigning clear ownership, establishing specific timelines, and defining success. This maintains momentum and ensures good ideas become a reality.

Finally, maintain momentum through consistent follow-through. Schedule regular check-ins to track progress, celebrate wins, and quickly address obstacles. Be prepared to adjust course based on learning while keeping sight of your ultimate objectives.

As you implement these principles, choose methods that fit your context and culture. Strategic summits serve well for broad transformation efforts, while innovation workshops excel at solving specific challenges. Design sprints help rapidly prototype solutions.[75] Most organizations benefit from combining approaches based on their particular needs and goals.

This systematic approach to co-creation generates more than solutions— it builds the foundation for sustained engagement and continuous improvement. When teams experience the power of creating together, they naturally become more innovative, collaborative, and purpose-driven.

Craft a High-Level Plan

As you develop your transformation plan, you will want to leverage best practices and break it down into manageable time frames.

We have drawn deeply from the large body of work on effective leadership,[76] [77] including the critical first 90-100 days.[78] In addition, we have augmented this with our own experiences working with executives facing new challenges. In the appendix, we share the detailed construct for a 100-day plan.

In the first month, focus on understanding the organization's priorities, essential players, internal dynamics, and external drivers. In month two, build strong relationships, align the team, refine workflows, and identify early wins. By month three, clarify and align on your mandate, establish guiding principles, and map out strategic shifts to drive impact, laying the groundwork for long-term transformation.

Appendix 3B offers a structured framework to ensure clarity and alignment in achieving objectives. It guides you in defining specific goals for each focus area, ensuring that efforts are purpose-driven and measurable. Setting priorities and timelines streamlines decision-making and resource allocation. The approach also emphasizes identifying important actions and milestones to track progress effectively. Lastly, it provides a continuous monitoring and adjustment system, allowing flexibility and course correction to stay on track. Such a framework will ensure your plan is both comprehensive and actionable.

While your transformation journey may be longer than 90 days, you will want to ensure that you consistently deliver measurable progress. If this is your first three months, it is even more critical as you are building a reputation. As a result, you should also have a personal plan laid out in 30-day increments.

By clarifying your mandate, aligning your vision, and engaging your team in co-creation, you've built a strong foundation for transformation. This thoughtful approach ensures that your leadership isn't just about quick wins but about sustainable impact that serves your organization's purpose. With these elements in place, you're ready to make the investments to drive success, which we'll explore in Part II.

Key Chapter Takeaways

- Establish clear priorities and focus areas, and avoid taking on too much.
- Rather than boiling the ocean, craft the plan in achievable chunks, balancing longer-term transformation and shorter-term goals.
- Co-create your plans to ensure alignment, engagement, and, ultimately, better results.
- Actively manage organizational politics.

Chapter 3 Reflection Questions

1. What does success look like in your role after one year?
2. How will you know if you're making meaningful progress?
3. What potential obstacles might derail your vision?
4. Who needs to be involved in co-creating the path forward?

PART II

Make Investments that Drive Success

Having established your foundation with a clear purpose, deep understanding, and compelling vision, it's time to make the investments to drive success. The following chapters focus on building the framework that will enable extraordinary results.

Chapter 4

Deepen Your Team's Connection to Purpose

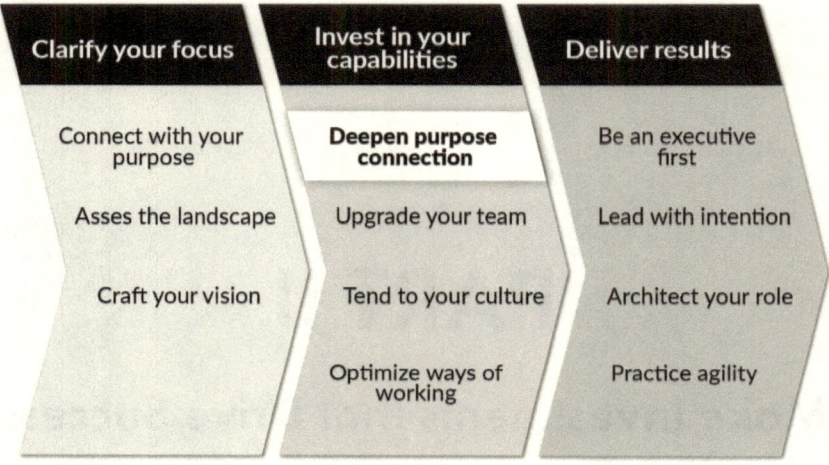

Clarify your focus	Invest in your capabilities	Deliver results
Connect with your purpose	**Deepen purpose connection**	Be an executive first
Asses the landscape	Upgrade your team	Lead with intention
Craft your vision	Tend to your culture	Architect your role
	Optimize ways of working	Practice agility

"He who has a why to live for can bear almost any how."
—Friedrich Nietzsche[79]

If you reflect on the guiding values and vision you established in Part I, you articulated what matters most. This chapter is about creating the conditions that support that vision and those values and keep you and your team connected to that purpose with meaningful work.

Transform Everyday Tasks into Meaningful Impact

"We choose to go to the Moon in this decade and do the other things, not because they are easy, but because they are hard; because that goal will serve to organize and measure the best of our energies and skills, because that challenge is one that we are willing to accept, one we are unwilling to

postpone, and one we intend to win," — President JFK, speech at Rice University, September 12, 1962[80]

As the story goes, when President John F. Kennedy was touring NASA in 1961, he introduced himself to a janitor who was mopping the floor and asked him what he did at NASA. The janitor responded, "...I'm helping put a man on the moon." Whether urban legend or not is beside the point; it is illustrative of the power of a singular and powerful purpose. That greater calling has a powerful impact to excite and empower every individual, regardless of their job.

Your role as a leader is to lay a foundation that will make conditions ripe for connecting to purpose, enabling you and your team to link daily tasks to support something larger than themselves. This chapter explores how to create a meaningful and sustainable work environment for you and the rest of your team. Specifically, we explore ways to align purpose with daily work and support autonomy at individual and team levels.

Later, in Chapter 5, we'll explore how 'job crafting' - thoughtfully adapting roles to increase meaning - can further enhance this connection. Specifically, we explore ways to support the alignment of purpose/inspiration and individual and collective autonomy in job crafting to maximize meaningfulness.

Nietzsche hit upon something magical when he articulated how important it is to us as human beings to tap into purpose. Would anyone you know sign up for a job that allowed them nearly no personal freedom for at least a year, forced them to rearrange their whole lives, and paid nothing?

Of course not!

But every day, thousands of people accept that job when they become parents. Olympic athletes across the globe make similar choices, putting vast amounts of time, money, effort, and sacrifice into unpaid endeavors. Similarly, volunteers passionate about a particular cause may contribute countless hours.

Why?

Because they know their efforts and sacrifices serve a greater purpose that holds significant meaning to them.

We are not suggesting that these endeavors are the same as work. But they do illustrate that humans happily put in a great deal of effort to serve something they are committed to. We can find many examples of the ability of some greater purpose driving motivation, engagement, and willingness to go the extra mile. While charitable giving, organ donation, and community service illustrate obvious linkages between purpose and motivation, the linkage doesn't necessarily need to be extreme to build meaning and drive discretionary effort.

Even less grandiose purposes can be motivational. Disney park employees experience a strong connection to helping make it a place for people to make memories. Entrepreneurial teams experience it as they build new companies. Stagehands connect to the mission of creating memorable performances. Customer support agents find satisfaction in knowing they have solved someone's problems. Chefs take pleasure in feeding hungry diners delicious meals. The purpose need not be life-saving or world-changing to be meaningful. As we discussed earlier, anyone in the organization, from the janitor to the CEO, can benefit from connection to purpose.

Academic research from a variety of perspectives[81] has substantiated the strong link between purpose and performance.[82] [83] [84] Simon Sinek and Frederic Laloux argue that connecting to a core purpose inspires teams and individuals.[85] As a result, organizations that build a strong connection between the work that they do and their core purpose motivate greater loyalty and unlock higher performance among their personnel.[86] While non-profits such as the World Health Organization, Heifer International, and World Vision have a purpose at the core of their DNA, every organization has the potential to build strong connections to its purpose.

As we discussed in Part I, USAA is one organization that, for over 100 years, has connected deeply to its purpose. They invest in keeping that connection alive through ongoing activities that intentionally integrate their mission into everything they do, from everyday happenings like meetings to social activities and service-based volunteer programs. USAA employs thousands of people in finance, HR, and other functions that never interact directly with the military members they serve. Despite that, these employees feel that purpose-driven connection and report that it gives them greater satisfaction in their work, motivates them to give extra effort, and builds a deeper connection and loyalty to the company.

Leaders who foster a strong connection between their teams and the organization's purpose do so in two critical ways. First, they inspire connection to and passion for the organization's purpose. Second, they build an understanding of how their specific roles and responsibilities contribute to delivering that purpose today and how they will improve it in the future. Being purpose-driven enables the team to see the value they create more effectively and embrace the work required to deliver it. As explorers, marathoners, and mountain climbers know, it's not the hard work that drives you forward but the view from the finish line or summit that inspires you to find satisfaction in the hard work it requires.

Work meaningfulness is not something we feel all the time; it is often episodic - ebbing and flowing as our work, moods, and conditions shift. The ongoing journey toward meaningful work is a dance that occurs for each of us in our work as we seek to draw meaning from it.

We are sense-making creatures and live and work in socially constructed worlds that must be nurtured. Because of this, words matter - *a lot*. The words we and others use to describe our roles and jobs help us make sense of what we do and connect it to the purpose we draw from it. This janitor re-cast his job of mopping the floor as doing his part in getting a man to the moon. It became meaningful rather than mundane work simply because he was a part of accomplishing something extraordinary. As leaders, we need to set the right tone, provide that worldview of context and meaning, and use ways of describing work that make that purpose-connection possible.

Cultivate Conditions for Meaningful Work

To maximize your performance and your team's, you must create an environment where they and you can find meaning. Work meaningfulness differs for each person; what one person may find meaningful, another person may not. This, and the fact that there are multiple dimensions to work meaningfulness, can make it a challenging concept to nurture or capture. Because we are all uniquely wired, the significance work holds for each of us is unique. There are several pathways, adapted from the work of Lips-Wiersma, that contribute to work meaningfulness, including:

- **Purpose / Inspiration:** Source of (and connection to) inspiration or purpose - this is anything that inspires. It could be a connection to a cause, family, or loved ones, and/or faith/spirituality.
- **Authenticity**: Having integrity with yourself and the ability to express your full potential - This is the degree to which you can be your authentic self at work, and the level of work taps into your gifts and skills.
- **Service**: Service to others - This is the connection they experience in serving a greater cause or simply serving those with whom their work intersects (e.g., customers, colleagues, community members).
- **Unity:** Unity with others - This is the degree to which they feel in sync with their co-workers [87]

One cautionary note is that, as we all know, there must be balance. Research shows that we are at our best when we balance being and doing (being/doing balance) and focus on ourselves and others (self/other balance). For example, practicing Yoga is a great habit. But if all you ever do is Yoga, you will be out of balance, negatively affecting your sense of having a meaningful life.

Similarly, if you work in a high-stress job serving others and do not adequately recharge your batteries, your stress levels will increase, and your sense of meaningfulness will suffer. Unsurprisingly, overworked doctors, nurses, and teachers, for instance, may experience burnout that can overshadow a healthy connection to meaning. Your goals as an individual and a purpose-driven leader should be to maintain balance for yourself and your team while also creating healthy conditions for meaningful work.

Beyond the moral and ethical arguments for supporting meaningful work (which, we assert, should be reason enough), research shows it makes good business sense, delivering greater employee engagement, retention, productivity, health, and customer service levels. But beware, it cannot be something that is forced or faked. Consider, for instance, a tone-deaf employee engagement survey that serves only to rile people up. You can't simply survey yourself into more meaningful work. Your care for your employees must come from a genuine place, starting with the example you set and the culture you create.

Consider how one CEO we worked with transformed these concepts into concrete actions by proactively encouraging his team to align their daily work with the organization's broader purpose. Through structured conversations and intentional role design, he helped team members identify opportunities to increase meaning in their work while delivering greater value to the organization. You can apply similar principles through the following framework.

Establish a Purpose-Driven Cultural Foundation

Your cultural foundation will primarily be driven by the vision and values you establish and maintain. The degree to which you communicate and live them out will create the guardrails for your company culture. Your culture is continually built one action/decision at a time and is reflected in observable actions.

Want to know your culture? Look at how you hire, fire, celebrate, reward, share financials, incentivize your workforce, treat your customers, and address ethical issues. This is how your employees experience your culture, and no set of actions sends this message more powerfully than how you operate and make small decisions day in and day out.

Countless books have been written on each of these topics, and while we will say more about culture in Chapter 6, we do not intend to cover these areas in extensive detail. The main point of emphasis is the importance of being intentional about each one of these areas and how they align with your vision and values. Think about the relative priorities and consider how you might align with each of these. The more you can nurture and embed your purpose and values, the more securely they will take root within the organization and undergird the transformation you are executing.

A growing body of research and practice suggests that one of the best ways to do this is to establish a culture that celebrates and leverages your strengths. As management thought leader Peter Drucker contends, the central task of good leadership is to align strengths in ways that make a system's weaknesses irrelevant.

Once you've established this strong connection to purpose, engage your team in co-creating your shared future. In our experience (and the research supports this), we find that leaders who leverage generative forums (that focus on the possible and the positive) and exercises to co-create a path forward (well-grounded in their purpose) end up with a much more cohesive and committed team. In part, this is because people support what they help to create. But beyond that, teams typically can think bigger and imagine greater transformative possibilities than any individual when given the permission and freedom to do so. More simply, you can see it as crowdsourcing your approach.

Over the years, we have led numerous transformations, and by far, the most effective approach to creating a plan has been in large-scale meetings representing the whole system that leverage appreciative approaches.[88] While we have used other techniques, we have often found them less effective. Generative, co-creation processes help ensure that your plans do not simply become empty words on a wall or tasks on a project plan. These become the team's transformative focus because they helped breathe life into them.

The process of co-creation is most effective when leaders apply the following principles:

Principle 1: Set clear objectives and boundaries

Before bringing your team together to create the plan, your job as a leader is to have critical conversations and interactions to redefine the limits, share your teachable point of view, and ensure their portfolio of possibilities is sufficiently widened. You will want to have laid out the big-picture focus and goals so that your team can work on delivering them.

Your role is to frame the focus. The better you do this, the more successful the new vision and supporting plans will be. So, be sure to put in the upfront work to define that focus clearly. Consider JFK's call to "put a man on the moon." He set the aim high, focused them on one target (the moon), and then got out of the way.

A technology executive we worked with transformed her organization's approach to innovation by reframing the challenge. Instead of dictating technical solutions, she asked her team: "How might we create an environment where every team member can contribute to breakthrough customer experiences?" This possibility-focused question invited broader participation and sparked creative thinking across all levels of the organization. By focusing on opportunities rather than problems, she helped her teams envision a future where innovation wasn't just the domain of senior architects but could emerge from anyone with customer insight.

The power of her approach lay not in prescribing solutions but in creating space for collective imagination. She established guardrails - like maintaining system reliability and security - while encouraging teams to dream bigger about how technology could serve their customers. This balance between clear direction and open exploration set the stage for meaningful co-creation with her team.

Principle 2: Engage Your Team

You have an opportunity to leverage the power of your team, harnessing their collective strengths. While many organizations tend to focus on root causes of failure and management by exception, we suggest an approach that has the power to transform. Borrowing from strengths-based practices, studying people and organizations at their best allows you to uncover "root causes of success." This becomes a positive driving force for the organization, which can propel it forward in ways that more antiquated fear-based, command and control-type management models fail to replicate.

From these identified success factors, the group can coalesce around a shared vision and imagine a bold new future built upon their strengths. In the case of newer organizations and teams without significant history, the team can draw upon other past experiences as they identify their strengths. Past wins, even at different organizations, also provide excellent case studies to identify the sources of potential success. The essential element here is understanding individual strengths and how they can unite as a whole system to build an incredible and synchronized team.

Consider a championship rowing team. When the rowers are perfectly synchronized, their collective power translates into smooth, efficient forward motion. That kind of teamwork is incredible because it feels as if every ounce of effort you put in as an individual is magnified tenfold across the boat. However, even slight misalignment between team members creates drag that, while barely noticeable to an observer, can make the boat feel heavy and slow. That drag compounds over time and ultimately determines the outcome of the race.

Organizations operate similarly. Small misalignments in purpose or execution may not immediately impact performance, but they significantly drag on results over time. As a leader, your role isn't to control every motion but to create the conditions for synchronicity - ensuring shared purpose, clear rhythm, and collective commitment. Success comes not from command-and-control but from every team member being fully aligned with and committed to the mission.

This can be accomplished by taking a positive, strengths-based approach that calls for leader humility and authenticity. And here's the genuinely liberating thing—you do not need to have all the answers! Surround yourself with good people and invite them into the process. Align the vision, figure out what support they need to do their best work, and then don't stand in their way.

Principle 3: Encourage brainstorming to generate possibilities

When brainstorming with your team, encourage them to dream big, rooting their ideas in factors that have contributed to prior successes.

Rather than censoring and constraining ideas at this stage, create an environment that supports creative thinking and builds upon collective strengths. It is helpful to utilize design thinking principles. Design thinking best practices call for us to move to action, deferring judgment to build upon the ideas of others (see Appendix 4A for additional information).

Great leaders do not have all the answers. Instead, they establish clear direction while creating the space and processes enabling teams to shape their shared future. During these sessions, team members are invited to dream big for themselves and the organization.

This allows for generative thinking otherwise inhibited by censorship and judgment in typical problem-solving approaches. Think about the times in your life when you have been asked to solve a problem. What tends to happen? If you are trained in traditional problem-solving methodologies like most, your mind fixates on a narrow cadre of possible solutions.

But if you think about it, for instance, when you were a child and let your imagination run wild, before you were adult enough to judge yourself and worry about conformity, you could come up with some pretty amazing ideas. This is about recapturing that spirit and creating an environment that allows these juices to flow. This generative thinking ultimately opens the company to new, previously unimagined possibilities.

As you consider the external opportunities available to your organization, evaluate all the external factors that affect the business, but consider them within the context of your purpose.

Putting Purpose into Practice

While purpose discussions can sometimes feel abstract, practical exercises help teams connect purpose to daily work. Consider three approaches that successful leaders have used:

1. Purpose Discovery Workshops

Bringing teams together for structured reflection helps uncover shared purpose and values. Through individual reflection, small group discussion, and collective integration, teams surface common themes that drive their best work and most significant impact.

2. Purpose-Impact Mapping

Regular assessment of how activities connect to purpose helps teams prioritize effectively. By mapping current work against purpose and impact, teams identify opportunities to create more value and eliminate low-impact activities.

3. Customer Impact Stories

Sharing specific examples of customer impact makes the purpose tangible. Regular sharing of these stories helps teams understand their value creation and identify opportunities for more significant impact.

For example, a software development team transformed their daily standups by adding purpose connection questions like "How does today's work impact users?" This simple change improved code quality and team engagement. Similarly, a customer service department added purpose metrics alongside traditional performance measures, resulting in higher customer loyalty and more innovative solutions.

[See Appendix 4B for detailed exercise guides and implementation tools.]

Case Study: Transformation of a Marketing Firm

One of our clients was a growing marketing firm that lost a major client and suffered a significant cash flow issue. If it were not fixed, they only had about 6 months before closing shop. They made the difficult but necessary decision to let several of their staff members go. They did so with a significant focus on preserving the dignity of each person in their conversations and providing transition support. One of their employees was actually relieved when she received the news because she felt such a sense of loyalty and was trying to tough things out, but she was deep down feeling called to something else.

With their remaining staff, they called an all-team workshop where they re-imagined operations for the entire day. There was a high degree of transparency and integrity as they opened up the books and discussed their business challenges. While their immediate focus was reducing costs, they also focused on capturing top-line revenue opportunities. They intentionally embraced an abundance (opportunity) mindset rather than a scarcity (cost-containment only) mindset.

The tone and energy of the meeting enabled creativity with new ideas, affirmation of the good work they were doing with their other satisfied customers, and figuring out how to address this challenge— TOGETHER. So, they all rolled up their sleeves and co-created a vision of their future and a plan to achieve it. While not erased, the anxiety around the necessary layoffs was undoubtedly lessened.

When done right, strengths-based, positive approaches do not ignore or sweep challenges under the rug. Instead, they acknowledge them and elevate thinking to prevent getting stuck in a negative, self-perpetuating downward spiral. This then opens a whole new level of performance that was previously unattainable.

In this case, the assembled team identified many new revenue streams and product/service innovations. These extended opportunities with new clients offered both immediate and longer-term options that they could implement. More importantly, the team was able to move beyond fear and anxiety with positive and constructive energy around the possibilities.

The company pulled itself out of this challenging period and is now thriving. This approach and intentional commitment to a better future made all the difference. It started with a mindful, collective discovery process, where they took stock of all the exceptional things they were already capable of and could double down on. Then, they charted their course together.

Following an appreciative, generative process allows your team to develop creative and actionable ideas that are often missed through more traditional problem-solving and planning methodologies. Once these generative ideas have been put on the table, people can collectively coalesce around them to create a shared vision. Since they have created this vision, they are now invested in making it a reality. Making them a reality requires a supportive cultural foundation for this process.

While a shared purpose creates alignment, you need the right team to bring it to life. Let's explore how to build and upgrade your team to deliver on your vision.

Key Chapter Takeaways

- Create a meaningful work environment supporting autonomy and focusing on purpose.
- People support what they help create, so engage the team with co-creation.
- Co-create a plan that brings the purpose to life, delivers on it, and drives strategic growth.

Chapter 4 Reflection Questions

1. How does your team's work connect to the larger organizational purpose?
2. What makes work meaningful for each of your team members?
3. Where do you see disconnects between stated purpose and daily work?
4. How can you better support individual team members in finding meaning in their work?

Chapter 5

Upgrade your winning team

Clarify your focus	Invest in your capabilities	Deliver results
Connect with your purpose	Deepen purpose connection	Be an executive first
Asses the landscape	**Upgrade your team**	Lead with intention
Craft your vision	Tend to your culture	Architect your role
	Optimize ways of working	Practice agility

"To go fast, go alone. To go far, go together."
—African proverb

Exceptional performance is built upon a team—not just any team, but a winning team. Upgrading to a winning team involves ensuring you've got the right people with the right talent and setting them up for success with a great culture that you consistently reinforce. It is a simple formula, but a non-trivial task.

Play As A Team

Anyone who followed the meteoric rise of the Chicago Bulls during the 1990s and their six championships during the Michael Jordan era might forget the struggles in Jordan's early tenure in the years prior. During the late 80s to early 90s, Jordan was essentially a one-man show. There were numerous games where his sheer will and drive delivered the win. The problem is that this was not scalable and could only carry a team so far. As soon as teams figured out how to double-team him during the playoff rounds, they quickly snuffed out the Bulls' chances to win.

During their first championship season, Jordan finally learned to pass the ball when he was hitting a wall instead of merely working to plow through or around it. When interviewed years later during the "Last Dance" ESPN series aired in 2020, Jordan retrospectively observed that Jackson admonished Jordan to look for Paxson, who was wide open when Jordan was double-teamed. Jordan finally released the ball to Paxson, who sank a three in the game's final minutes, winning the game and clinching the NBA championship.

Jordan's journey from individual superstar to championship team leader parallels the evolution many executives must make. Just as Jordan had to learn that trusting Paxson with crucial shots strengthened the team, executives must recognize that empowering their team members often leads to better outcomes than making every decision themselves. The Bulls' six championships weren't just about having the greatest player - they were about having a leader who learned to leverage the full potential of his team. Similarly, extraordinary organizational performance emerges when executives shift from being star individual contributors to true team leaders.

This pattern plays out countless times in organizations where leaders struggle to make this same transition. Despite the evidence that teams outperform individuals, many executives still try to do it all themselves, dictating from the top-down rather than engaging their team. It seems obvious, yet this lesson often has to be learned the hard way.

But an all-too-common scenario plays out in organizations of all sizes as they lose sight of this. A company leader identifies a potential opportunity; arguably, it's a stroke of genius. It delivers a critical pivot for the company and could position it for massive growth in the market. The leader draws up the concept and shares it with their peers. They think it is great and agree to move forward on it. So far, so good, right?

The problem is that they move out with their new plans but never communicate or engage the folks on the frontlines of the organization. Instead, they build momentum, gearing up for the big reveal. And that's when the surprises happen, and chaos ensues. They discover too late that there are unforeseen problems - maybe features are not compatible with existing offerings, or it cannot be manufactured on existing equipment at the target price, or any number of other things that could have been foreseen had they gotten input from a wider swath of the organization. All could have been prevented by engaging individuals from product, services, sales, etc. The idea has the potential to provide a significant breakthrough for the company. Still, it is now a major disaster, wasting time and valuable resources and causing rework and stress. What went wrong?

Research tells us that the most complex and wicked problems and the most elegant and innovative solutions are created not by a sole individual genius but by great collaborators who bring different perspectives. The Chilean mine rescue, the Olympic victory of the 1980s "Miracle on Ice" team, and the Apple iPod launch—yep, you guessed it—were all team efforts. Delivering long-term success and overcoming challenging situations requires a fully engaged team's expertise, creativity, and hard work.

While sports teams provide clear examples of collective achievement, similar patterns of team excellence emerge across diverse industries. Consider these examples:

Healthcare

At Mayo Clinic, physician-led teams combine research, education, and patient care in a unique model that consistently ranks among the world's best healthcare providers.[89] Their success stems from balancing individual expertise with collective decision-making. Each patient benefits from "integrated practice units" where specialists collaborate rather than working in silos. This approach has delivered both superior patient outcomes and breakthrough medical innovations.[90]

Manufacturing

Toyota's production system demonstrates how front-line teams drive organizational excellence. Their teams are empowered to stop production lines when quality issues arise - a radical departure from traditional manufacturing approaches.[91] More importantly, their kaizen (continuous improvement) system enables any team member to suggest improvements. This resulted in over 40 million implemented suggestions since the program's inception, driving Toyota's industry-leading quality and efficiency.[92]

Technology

Spotify revolutionized team organization with its "squad" model, where small, cross-functional teams operate with high autonomy while maintaining alignment with company objectives.[93] Each squad owns a distinct portion of the user experience and can make independent decisions about implementation. This balance of autonomy and alignment has enabled Spotify to innovate rapidly while scaling globally.

Public Sector

FEMA's crisis response teams demonstrate excellence under extreme pressure. Their ability to rapidly form effective teams from diverse agencies and maintain high performance in chaotic situations comes from clear protocols combined with adaptive leadership.[94] During Hurricane Katrina recovery, teams processed over 2.5 million applications for assistance while coordinating responses across multiple states.

These examples demonstrate the power of the team. However, building a great team requires having the right talent. Like successful theatre productions, casting the right team members in the right roles is crucial.

Cast Well

You need three things in the theatre — the play, the actors and the audience, and each must give something."
—Kenneth Haigh[95]

As you consider moving forward with the plan, you must also examine your team. Do you have the right skills, capabilities, and mindsets? As Collins famously said in his book *Good to Great*, you need to get the right people on the bus for this journey.[96] Build out your "A" team, thinking through who will contribute what, who might not be a long-term fit, and who you might need to add to the team.

One of Patrick's favorite pastimes is performing in and watching good theatre. Part of his love for theatre stems from the fact that it provides such valuable lessons in leadership. The theatre offers some great principles as we focus on what makes for a high-performing team that consistently delivers excellent performances.

Just as a theatre director must look beyond individual talent to consider ensemble chemistry, executives must build teams where skills and styles complement each other. A brilliant leading actor can't carry a show alone - they need supporting players who enhance their performance while bringing their unique strengths to the production. Similarly, even the most talented executive needs team members who can both support and challenge them.

The rehearsal process in theatre, like organizational onboarding and development, is where individual talents merge into collective excellence. Directors don't just assign roles and hope for the best - they carefully cultivate understanding, build relationships, and create an environment where everyone can do their best work. Successful executives take the same approach, investing time in helping their team members understand their roles and how they fit into the larger production of organizational success.

Even if you have a rockstar team member, they alone cannot carry the whole show. Aligning team members and their respective strengths enables you to set the stage for an optimal performance. Hiring well also means hiring for diversity of perspectives, skills, and life experiences. If disregarded, typecasting the same leads, you run the risk of having a monotonous performance that is stale and lacks vitality. Furthermore, you fail to develop new talent with fresh perspectives and capabilities.

While it may seem like a safe choice to cast only known quantities - those you've worked with before - restricting yourself to only those players can cost you the opportunity to innovate, push boundaries, and deliver something truly spectacular.

As a leader, carefully assess your team's skills and strengths. Then, consider the hard work ahead of them. Is there an opportunity to add or trade resources to set your projects up for better success? Think like a great director, looking to create not merely a collection of talented individuals, but an ensemble that brings out the best in each other.

There's no way around it. Successful shows have a great cast. This means choosing carefully and assessing individuals' skills, passions, and perspectives. It is not so different from hiring. Putting someone in a leading role can be disastrous if they can't play it well. In the best case, the show (project) will be a slog. In the worst case, the performance (project) will bomb. The same thing is true when hiring. An incompetent or toxic team member can become a dead weight or, worse, a cancer that must be addressed.

Extraordinary performance requires individual excellence and seamless collaboration, whether on the basketball court or the theatre stage. The same holds in organizations - success comes not from having a collection of stars but from building a team that can work together to deliver results beyond what any individual could achieve alone. This understanding should guide not only how we select talent but also how we develop and support them once they're on board.

As a leader, your role resembles a director assembling a cast. First, assess your current team's skills and strengths against the challenges ahead. Look for opportunities to add complementary talents or develop existing team members into new roles. Consider creating a wish list of both hard skills (technical expertise, industry experience) and soft skills (coaching, leadership) that would strengthen your ensemble.

How you conduct it is just as significant as the casting process itself. Your hiring practices should reflect your values and organizational culture. A disrespectful casting call that subjects actors to poor treatment will repel top talent; similarly, broken recruiting processes can damage your brand and deter great candidates. This is especially true for internal roles and promotions, where your practices directly impact team culture and morale.

Onboard Well

Once you've made casting (hiring) decisions, it's crucial to consider your onboarding processes. It's common to do a read-through with the entire cast when casting a new show. This allows cast members to acquaint themselves with the whole piece, meet their castmates, and hear the director's perspectives, vision, and additional context. Similarly, acclimating new team members to your core mission, values, and processes doesn't just happen by osmosis. Consider how you acquaint or reacquaint your team with your vision. Wherever possible, establish standard processes and engage team members to build ownership in the design and delivery of onboarding processes with new staff.

A cast shares the common purpose of putting on a high-quality production. In the same way, your team has shared goals, though sometimes they are implied. Make them explicit. Grounding the team in your organization's key objectives and results is time well spent.

As a leader, surround yourself with good people, delegate well, and give people room to work. If you've done the hard work upfront in aligning vision, purpose, goals, job design/accountabilities, and metrics, you can allow people to do the work you hired them to do more fully. This will create a more meaningful experience for them and have a direct positive impact on outcomes such as engagement, productivity, and retention, which all have direct and indirect effects on the bottom line. To help encourage coachability as a leader, model openness to feedback. Sometimes, your actors/team members may have an inspired idea you hadn't considered as a director/leader. It starts with being willing to admit that you don't (and won't) have all the answers. Keep an open mind where warranted, and then act decisively once you make a decision.

When individuals bring a spirit of humility, curiosity, and openness, actors/team members have better experiences and produce better results. Conversely, working with a diva is a miserable experience, often resulting in sub-optimal performance. The same is true when you have divas on your team at work. Not only will your employees suffer, but so will your customers and your results.

While building strong team relationships and collaboration is essential, you also need systems that reinforce and sustain these cultural elements. How you measure and reward performance plays a crucial role in shaping team behavior and culture.

Align Performance Metrics with Culture

Like a good director shares their vision regularly and openly, good leaders maintain transparency around performance metrics and goals. Many organizations use balanced scorecards or similar frameworks to provide teams with a clear line of sight to how their work impacts overall success. These include traditional financial metrics and track customer satisfaction, operational excellence, and employee development measures. Some leaders take this transparency further through practices like open-book management, sharing detailed financial data to foster an ownership mindset.

[For more on implementing balanced performance measurement systems, see Kaplan & Norton's work on balanced scorecards or Stack's Great Game of Business for open-book management approaches.]

For example, one food industry client developed a comprehensive, balanced scorecard that connected individual and team contributions directly to organizational success. They tracked financial performance, customer impact, process improvement, and capability development. This holistic approach helped team members understand how their daily work contributed to broader organizational goals and enabled more informed decision-making at all levels.

Then, align your performance metrics to support the culture and goals you wish to drive. We once worked in an organization where the sales team was heavily remunerated on reaching revenue targets but lacked accountability for profitability. You can imagine the results - a "sales at any cost" culture resulted in sales that became toxic as it competed with the company's best interests. There was such pressure to sell that several large deals resulted in a net financial loss to the company. Additionally, sales pressures overwhelmed company values, resulting in some deals not being in the customers' best interest. As such, it's essential to ensure that you are setting up appropriate incentives supported by the right metrics and working to maintain constructive friction between your values and incentives.

With your performance metrics aligned to support your desired culture, you can focus on creating the environment that enables your team to thrive. High-performing teams regularly reflect on how they work together, not just what they produce. They create structured opportunities to experiment with new approaches to collaboration and communication. The most effective teams make this reflection process a natural part of their rhythm, continuously evolving how they leverage each member's strengths and address challenges together.

Tap into Meaning

As we have already discussed, nothing is more potent than a team of people who work in harmony toward a goal, and that team, when working together, can do more than you could ever do as an individual. Rather than trying to undertake this effort on your own as their "leader," instead, lean into the "we" of teamwork and create it together. Your solution will not only be better but will have the added benefit of having the team's buy-in because they helped create it. It's the only way to sustain a repeatable competitive advantage.

Architect for maximum engagement by tapping into the meaning we discussed in the last chapter, and consider what each member of your team finds most meaningful in their work. If they relish interacting with your customers, find ways to maintain and scale that. If they relish getting into the numbers, find ways to leverage that. Conversely, if there is something that sucks their soul, look for ways to reallocate that work and build systems to take this work off their plate where feasible.

Consider reflecting on the core elements of Lips-Wiersma's Map of Meaningful Work[97] to understand better areas to emphasize or identify gaps. This reflection exercise, available in Appendix 5A, can help you and your team explore these dimensions thoughtfully and at your comfort level. Remember that such exploration should always be by invitation - team members should feel free to engage with these concepts at their own pace and depth.

Also, consider workshopping these reflection questions with your team members individually and as a group, to the extent of their comfort, to assess the areas that bring them the most significant work meaningfulness. It can be helpful to reflect upon a given period (e.g., the past week, quarter, or year) to consider what aspects contributed (or detracted from) their work meaningfulness. This practice could be integrated into your reviews or retrospectives for lean shops.

Connected to this idea of understanding what creates meaning for each team member, consider creating what Adam Grant and other leadership experts call 'User Manuals' - personal operating guides that make explicit the often implicit aspects of how we work best. These guides help team members understand each other's preferences, work styles, and energy sources. For example, you might share that you're a morning person who does best with strategic thinking before noon or prefers direct communication over hints. Making these preferences explicit builds psychological safety and rapport while reducing the guesswork in team interactions.

When leaders model this transparency by creating and sharing their user manual first, it establishes permission for authentic sharing across the team. This practice can significantly reduce friction in team interactions while deepening understanding and trust. It's particularly valuable during onboarding or team formation, but can be introduced anytime to enhance team dynamics. (See Appendix 5B for detailed guidelines and examples.)

Consider what actions might leverage these insights once you've reflected upon them for yourself and/or your team. One method of doing this is through a practice called job crafting. Job crafting is the practice of customizing job responsibilities around the edges of a formal job description to tailor responsibilities in ways that build meaning. If this were a sports team, you would think of this as optimizing each person's role so that each member plays optimally and you maximize the overall team performance. Think of how Christian Ronaldo (the world-famous football/soccer player) bloomed as a player when he moved from wing to central striker, or how players came together to rise to the occasion, such as Argentina's Basketball dominance of a USA team of professional superstars to capture Olympic gold in 2004.

Support "Job Crafting"

The concept of job crafting was developed by organizational psychologists Wrzesniewski and Dutton, who studied hospital cleaning staff and discovered how individuals shaped their roles to create greater meaning.[98] Though they all shared the same job description, they experienced vastly different degrees of work meaningfulness depending on how they viewed their jobs. As the janitor JFK spoke to at NASA, janitors working in hospitals who viewed their job as helping patients heal found more meaning in their work.

Finding real meaning and connecting it to a purpose compelled them to lean into tasks beyond their job descriptions. They spoke with patients in comas, moved pictures to try to change stimuli, and comforted family members. Their ability to transform their job in ways that fed their souls was powerful. Though not in the scope of the original study, it is not a leap to hypothesize that this had positive ripples for the patients and their families, co-workers, and the general goodwill of the hospital. Consider the transformative impact of small changes, not just within hospitals but across all workplaces.

As the leader, you must walk the walk here, adopting and encouraging finding meaning in work. As a starting point, allow yourself to be authentic and vulnerable in your journey towards creating meaningful work experiences. Model and inspire it for your employees by sharing your process of discovering purpose in your role. For instance, start team meetings by highlighting moments where you've found unexpected meaning in routine tasks or openly discuss challenges you've faced in maintaining a connection to purpose during difficult periods. Create regular forums where team members can share their stories of finding meaning, whether through formal presentations or informal coffee chats.

When making decisions, verbalize how they connect to your team's broader purpose, explicitly linking daily actions and meaningful impact. Be transparent about your job crafting efforts—perhaps you've restructured your calendar to spend more time mentoring because you find it deeply meaningful, or redesigned a regular process to serve your team's purpose better. These authentic examples show your team that purpose-driven leadership isn't just theoretical—it's a practical, ongoing journey that starts with you.

Allowing people to "craft" their jobs by shifting and tweaking portions of their roles also creates a fertile ground for innovation that can drive exceptional outcomes.[99] Great leaders intentionally lean into job crafting by understanding their team members' strengths, weaknesses, desires, and passions, adjusting roles where possible, and encouraging others to do the same. They make meaningful changes and adjustments that ultimately improve both individual and organizational performance.[100] [101]

We previously discussed Drucker's insight about creating an alignment of strengths that makes weaknesses irrelevant. This principle applies perfectly to job crafting, where leaders actively assign roles and responsibilities in ways that connect to the organization's mission and values. When making these assignments, openly acknowledge this goal and involve your team in those discussions. Doing so will create a culture that recognizes the individual gifts that each person brings. This is about finding the highest and best use of everyone's strengths and skills as they deliver on the purpose. Look for opportunities to automate, eliminate, and delegate more routine tasks and allocate the remainder where they give the most joy.

Organizations that adopt a lean or agile approach do this routinely in their process reviews. They constantly experiment to find better and more effective ways to do things, and this practice becomes part of the organization's fiber.

Measure What Matters

While intuition about team performance is valuable, systematic measurement ensures sustainable excellence. Successful leaders develop comprehensive frameworks that assess both immediate performance and long-term capability building.[102]

Leading Indicators

These metrics help predict future success and identify areas needing attention before they impact results. Leading indicators include team engagement levels, decision-making velocity, and the frequency of cross-functional collaboration. Organizations also track their innovation pipeline health and knowledge-sharing effectiveness to spot potential issues early.

For example, Adobe tracks "checkpoint" conversations between managers and team members, measuring the frequency and quality of these interactions. This leading indicator helps predict team performance and retention.[103]

Lagging Indicators

Lagging indicators confirm whether your team is delivering desired results through metrics like project completion rates, quality measures, and customer satisfaction scores. They also include traditional business metrics such as employee retention, revenue impact, and market share growth.

DTE Energy found that teams with high purpose alignment delivered 23% higher customer satisfaction scores and contributed to a threefold increase in stock price over nine years.[104]

Process Metrics

Operational measures help optimize team effectiveness by tracking cycle time for pivotal deliverables, error and rework rates, and resource utilization. Teams also monitor response time to stakeholders and adoption rates for new changes. Cisco's high-performing teams, for instance, reduced their average project cycle time by 40% by measuring and optimizing their collaboration processes.[105]

Cultural Indicators

To assess organizational health, teams track cultural indicators, including psychological safety levels, trust indices, and purpose alignment. They also measure how well teams adhere to stated values and maintain a learning orientation.

Google's Project Aristotle found that psychological safety was the strongest predictor of team performance, leading them to implement regular measurement of team dynamics.[106]

Creating Your Measurement Framework

1. Select metrics that:
   - Align with your purpose and strategy
   - Balance short and long-term focus
   - Include both hard and soft measures
   - Are actionable at the team level

2. Establish regular review rhythms:
   - Daily/weekly operational metrics
   - Monthly performance reviews
   - Quarterly strategic assessments
   - Annual comprehensive evaluations

3. Use data to:
   - Guide improvement efforts
   - Inform resource allocation
   - Recognize achievement
   - Shape development plans

With clear metrics to guide your team's development, you can begin building your dream team.

Design Your Team's Path to Excellence

Begin by envisioning what truly exceptional performance looks like for your team. What combination of skills, capabilities, and ways of working will drive sustainable success? Rather than creating an exhaustive list, focus on the few critical elements that will make the most significant difference.

Start with your purpose and values as the foundation, then assess your current talent against these aspirations. Look beyond technical expertise to essential leadership qualities like work ethic, collaboration, and creativity. This holistic evaluation helps identify both strengths to leverage and gaps to address.

With this understanding, development paths can be created that serve individual growth and collective success. The goal isn't just to build individual capabilities but to create conditions for the team to excel.

Great teams have great cultures, and research has consistently shown specific principles that drive their success. In their seminal works *The Wisdom of Teams* and *The Discipline of Teams*,[107] [108] Katzenbach and Smith identified fundamental characteristics that distinguish high-performing teams: shared purpose, clear performance goals, complementary skills, mutual accountability, and a commitment to common working approaches. These elements create the foundation for what we've been discussing - a culture that enables extraordinary performance.

When these principles are combined with the purpose-driven elements we've explored, teams develop 'performance synergy.' They don't just collaborate effectively - they innovate, adapt, and consistently deliver beyond expectations. This happens because team members:

- Connect their individual purposes to the team's mission
- Feel psychologically safe to take risks and share ideas
- Support one another's growth and development
- Share credit and learn from mistakes
- Communicate transparently and authentically

Leaders who build such cultures do so intentionally, not just through what they say but through consistent actions and systems that reinforce these behaviors. They create forums for open dialogue, celebrate collective achievements over individual heroics, and ensure that their reward systems align with their stated values.

This culture becomes self-reinforcing. As team members experience the benefits of this approach, they naturally begin to model and promote these behaviors themselves. The result is a community of practice where continuous improvement and mutual support become the norm rather than the exception.

However, building such a culture requires more than just good intentions. You'll need to develop specific mechanisms that support and sustain these principles.

Consider developing a road map with your team's input that delineates how these shifts will be realized. As a reminder, it is far better to focus on a few strategic shifts done well than a large number done haphazardly. It takes time and buy-in to develop habits. Keep your scope modest and take an MVP approach where you can learn from what you apply and adapt as you go. In addition, look for leaders inside your team who model best practices to magnify your impact.

That roadmap becomes your talent and team development North Star, guiding your aspirational goals and daily decisions about people and performance. Your commitment to culture is demonstrated by the behaviors you tolerate, not the values you espouse. When you allow someone to consistently act counter to your desired culture, especially a high performer, you send a powerful message that undermines everything else you're trying to build. Your team will quickly recognize that your stated values are merely window dressing rather than true guiding principles.

When you allow someone to consistently act counter to your desired culture, you send a powerful message that undermines everything else you're trying to build.

This is why making tough personnel decisions about cultural misalignment, even with technically skilled performers, is essential for maintaining credibility as a leader. Your team needs you to make these difficult choices to enable their collective success.

This is easier said than done - we know. One of the companies we worked with had a chief architect who knew their software inside and out, and everyone thought they were too valuable to let go. But he was a hoarder of information and collaborated with no one, making it challenging to work with him. The CTO understood it was not a good fit with the culture they needed to build and ultimately decided to fire him. Everyone was shocked but relieved, as many shared that it was the moment they knew the culture mattered.

Fast forward a few years, and it turned out that the loss of knowledge and capabilities was minimal and temporary, while the resulting benefits were significant. Releasing that architect turned out to be a pivotal event in the transformation and ultimate success of the company. We have seen this time and time again, where leaders and companies fear the potential impact of removing a strategic but toxic resource, only to discover the cost was minimal and the benefits were immense.

The major lesson is that one star player is never more valuable than the collective potential of your team. You can replace individual skills (even though it may seem impossible), but you cannot overcome a toxic culture. In the next chapter, we will discuss more about the elements of an optimal team culture.

A strong team needs an equally strong community and culture to thrive. Building genuine kinship and collaboration takes your talented team from good to extraordinary.

Key Chapter Takeaways

- Hire smart and assign roles and jobs well so that you leverage and develop their talent.
- Think about every process and its implications, from hiring to firing to onboarding, meetings, space use, policies, and communication channels.
- Support each team member's connection to purpose and meaning.
- Optimize each team member's role, focusing on individual and team development.

- Be intentional about your choices, as those will ultimately shape your culture and team performance.

Chapter 5 Reflection Questions

1. What are the current strengths and gaps in your team?
2. How well does your team culture support high performance?
3. What development opportunities could help your team level up?
4. Where might you need to make difficult personnel decisions?

Chapter 6

Tend to Your Culture

Clarify your focus	Invest in your capabilities	Deliver results
Connect with your purpose	Deepen purpose connection	Be an executive first
Asses the landscape	Upgrade your team	Lead with intention
Craft your vision	**Tend to your culture**	Architect your role
	Optimize ways of working	Practice agility

"I used to believe that culture was 'soft,' and had little bearing on our bottom line. What I believe today is that our culture has everything to do with our bottom line, now and into the future." —Vern Dosch, author, Wired Differently

"Customers will never love a company until the employees love it first." —Simon Sinek, author, Start with Why[109]

Build a Strong Cultural Foundation

Culture change doesn't happen by declaring it. While many organizations launch formal "culture change initiatives," we've found through years of working with executives that the most successful cultural transformations happen more organically. Rather than focusing explicitly on changing culture, the most effective leaders create conditions for cultural evolution by:

1. Rallying their teams around a compelling shared vision
2. Getting everyone rowing in the same direction toward meaningful goals
3. Establishing clear guardrails that define acceptable behaviors and practices - both what is preferred and what is prohibited

Culture change doesn't happen by declaring it.

Think of culture as the natural outcome of how people work together to pursue shared objectives rather than something to be directly engineered. When teams are united in purpose and clear about expectations, positive cultural elements emerge and strengthen naturally. Your role as a leader is to create the conditions that allow this to happen while maintaining appropriate boundaries.

This approach is compelling because it grounds cultural development rather than abstract values in day-to-day work. When teams connect their daily activities to a meaningful purpose, behavioral changes emerge naturally rather than feeling forced. Success builds upon success as shared achievements create momentum. Throughout this process, the focus remains squarely on what matters most to the business - delivering value while building sustainable capabilities.

With this foundation in mind, let's explore the key elements that create fertile ground for a strong, purpose-driven culture.

Build Championship Culture

*Sports is such a great teacher. I think of everything they've
taught me: camaraderie, humility, how to resolve differences.*
—Kobe Bryant

With this understanding that culture emerges from shared purpose and collective action, let's examine how great teams put these principles into practice. Sports teams provide vivid examples of how culture develops through pursuing common goals while maintaining precise standards. From the time you onboard, it's imperative to articulate and reinforce the behaviors that will support your team's success. Take stock of where your team is on their 'culture creation' journey and what adjustments you may wish to make to realize your vision.

Don't leave this to chance. And don't fall into the trap of mistaking what Marcus Buckingham calls 'cultural plumage' - the ping pong tables, free snacks, and casual Fridays - for authentic culture.[110] While these perks might be nice additions, they're merely surface-level manifestations, not the substance of culture itself. Authentic culture lives in how work gets done, decisions get made, and how people treat each other in pursuit of shared goals. The culture you establish through these fundamental behaviors will determine your performance. The adage that culture eats strategy for breakfast is very true, so it's worth your focus.

An extraordinary example of how culture drives performance is the 2008 USA Olympic Basketball team (commonly referred to as "The Redeem Team"). This team faced a daunting comeback after the debacle of the 2004 USA Olympic loss to Argentina. Despite the surplus of talent of the USA 2004 team (essentially, hiring well), their lack of humility when playing together drove their poor performance.

Leading up to the 2008 games, Coach Mike Krzyzewski (Coach K.), the legendary Duke basketball coach, recognized that the team culture was the most important thing they had to change. Coach K, a former West Point Grad, invited Navy SEALS and military generals to talk to the team about the tremendous responsibility of serving and representing their country.

Superstar Kobe Bryant shared that this created a sense that this was their call to duty, "Our small way of representing the United States of America. You can play for the Los Angeles Lakers, you can play for the Spurs, the Heat, the Mavs, whoever, but it's different when you put on a USA jersey because now you're playing for [your] country." That connection to purpose – the principles we covered earlier in this chapter, as we discussed meaningfulness – was the beginning of the change, but it was only the first step.[111]

The second critical step Coach K. took was to bring the team together. He put them in the same hotel and on the same training schedule. This helped break down barriers and provide time for them to bond. It wasn't long before everyone noticed Kobe Bryant, long known for his incredible work ethic, waking up early to practice, and soon, others shifted their schedules to do the same.

Over time, more and more players would join Kobe for 5 am practice until most of the team showed up for what became known as the "Breakfast Club." Soon, it was not just early workouts but also shooting practice in the evenings, during which they built a strong camaraderie. This way, USA Basketball built a team culture of strong connection, smart play, and arduous work. More than anything else, that culture fueled their capabilities to reclaim Olympic Gold and earn the right to be called the Redeem Team.

Creating fertile ground for your vision and ambition to take hold requires real action to build the right culture. Consider the contrasting example of the 2004 USA Olympic Basketball "Dream Team." They were arguably the most naturally talented team in the world. But, talent without teamwork and collaboration was not enough to deliver on their potential. They hadn't come together as a unit.

As a result, they lacked a deep understanding of one another's strengths, weaknesses, and tendencies. They didn't have a feel for how their teammates played and reacted on the court together. Despite all their raw talent and horsepower, they did not bring home the gold. Why? They were still just a set of individual players because they had not developed the community and kinship to become a great team. Thanks to scoreboards, the performance of sports teams, both winners and losers, is easy to assess. But what about teams at work?

Harness Collective Strength

While star talent like the "Redeem Team" can drive success, sustainable excellence isn't just about assembling the most talented individuals. It is equally likely that at some point in your career, there was a less experienced team that had fewer resources and much less raw talent but delivered great things. These teams often succeed because they build strong communities with deep trust and collaboration. They compensate for individual limitations through collective strength, frequently developing innovative solutions precisely because they can't rely on overwhelming resources or expertise.

The significant differentiator for these teams typically isn't their individual capabilities but how they work together. High-performing teams build genuine trust and psychological safety, creating an environment where knowledge flows freely and continuous learning is the norm. Team members actively support each other through challenges while celebrating collective rather than individual achievements. Their shared commitment to mission consistently takes precedence over individual recognition.

Your experiences with high-performing teams likely reflect these patterns. Think about teams that truly excelled versus those that struggled - the difference often lies in how leadership enabled or inhibited collective success. Consider which cultural elements fostered collaboration and innovation and how recognition systems reinforced team achievement rather than individual accomplishment. These reflections can help you identify the specific practices and systems that build sustainable team excellence.

Team experiences have the most significant impact on an organization's culture.[112] Since most of our time is spent working in and through teams, this shapes our day-to-day cultural experiences.

Research by Buckingham and Goodall established eight factors that predict sustained team performance.[113] Members of high-performing teams consistently agree with the following eight statements, which align with those factors.

Best of "we"	Best of "me"
1. I am really enthusiastic about the mission of my company.	2. At work, I clearly understand what is expected of me.
3. In my team, I am surrounded by people who share my values.	4. I have the chance to use my strengths every day at work.
5. My teammates have my back.	6. I know I will be recognized for excellent work.
7. I have great confidence in my company's future.	8. In my work, I am always challenged to grow.

The odd questions (in the left column of the table above) above represent elements created by team members' shared, communal experience at work—the "best of we questions." The even questions (in the right column of the table above) are the "best of me experiences." The beauty of these statements is their simplicity and clarity. As a leader, you know what you need to focus on and can directly impact and influence how real they become in the daily work of your teams. Undergirding them, however, are some foundational elements of a healthy team culture, which we'll explore here.

Establish Your Cultural Cornerstones

Building a culture that continually fosters excellence at the individual and team levels is challenging. It is dependent on four foundational elements: **psychological safety, performance excellence, operational autonomy, and a growth focus**. We will take each in turn.

Foster Psychological Safety

In a psychologically safe environment, team members feel they can take interpersonal risks without fear of negative consequences. Harvard professor Amy Edmondson's research shows that psychological safety is crucial for team learning, innovation, and performance.[114] Google's extensive Project Aristotle research confirmed psychological safety as the most critical factor in team effectiveness.[115]

Psychological safety within a team is evident when members feel comfortable speaking up without fear of reprisal, fostering open communication and trust. Mistakes are treated as learning opportunities rather than sources of punishment, encouraging continuous improvement. Diverse perspectives are actively sought and valued, creating a culture where different viewpoints contribute to better decision-making. Team members feel free to ask questions without worrying about appearing incompetent, reinforcing a commitment to growth and knowledge-sharing. Instead of assigning blame, failures are examined for learning and improvement, strengthening individual and collective performance.

Leaders build psychological safety through specific but consistent actions, such as effectively framing the work, modeling openness, responding productively, and creating well-structured opportunities.

Effective leaders frame the work by emphasizing its complexity and inherent uncertainty, helping their teams understand that ambiguity is a natural part of the process. Rather than presenting obstacles as roadblocks, they position challenges as valuable learning opportunities, fostering a mindset of growth and adaptability. At the same time, they set clear expectations, providing direction and structure while openly acknowledging the unknowns. This balanced approach builds confidence, encourages problem-solving, and empowers teams to navigate uncertainty with resilience.

Modeling openness as a leader means admitting mistakes and openly sharing the lessons learned, creating an environment where growth is valued over perfection. Leaders build trust and encourage authenticity within their teams by showing vulnerability when appropriate. Demonstrating a willingness to learn from feedback reinforces a culture of continuous improvement, while expressing genuine curiosity about others' perspectives fosters collaboration and deeper understanding. This approach strengthens relationships and empowers teams to engage in honest dialogue and innovation.

Responding productively as a leader means creating an environment where openness is met with appreciation and constructive engagement. Thanking team members for speaking up, especially about problems, reinforces a culture of trust and psychological safety. When mistakes occur, responding with curiosity rather than blame encourages learning and problem-solving. Acknowledging and building on good ideas fosters innovation and collaboration while addressing concerns directly and transparently, ensuring that issues are resolved effectively. By responding this way, leaders cultivate a team dynamic rooted in respect, growth, and continuous improvement.

Creating structured opportunities for open dialogue and learning ensures that psychological safety becomes a consistent part of a team's culture. Regular forums for sharing concerns provide a dedicated space for honest conversations, while established processes for discussing failures help normalize learning from mistakes. Integrating feedback into regular workflows encourages continuous improvement and prevents critical insights from being overlooked. Additionally, making space for diverse perspectives fosters inclusivity and innovation, ensuring that all voices are heard and valued.

Psychological safety is particularly crucial for purpose-driven organizations because it enables authentic connection to shared purpose, supports innovation in service of mission, and creates space for meaningful work discussions. Research shows that when team members feel psychologically safe, they're more likely to engage in the kind of risk-taking and experimentation that leads to breakthrough performance.[116]

To assess the level of psychological safety in your team, consider these indicators:

Indicator	Key questions
Observable Behaviors	• How often do team members speak up in meetings? • Do people readily share mistakes and lessons learned? • Is dissent expressed directly or only in private? • Do junior members challenge senior members' ideas?
Team Dynamics	• How are new ideas received? • How does the team handle failure? • What happens when someone makes a mistake? • How are differences of opinion managed?
Leadership Indicators	• Do you hear bad news quickly? • Do people come to you with problems? • Is feedback flowing in all directions? • Are questions welcomed and addressed?

Building psychological safety requires consistent attention and practice.

To help you evaluate psychological safety in your organization, we've provided a set of reflection questions in Appendix 6B. These questions are designed for leaders and team members to assess current practices and identify opportunities for improvement. Considering these questions thoughtfully can reveal vital insights about your team's psychological safety climate and highlight specific areas for development.

With psychological safety established as your foundation, teams can fully engage in performance excellence, knowing they have the support to take appropriate risks and learn from both successes and failures.

Expect High Standards of Performance

High-performance standards are closely tied to the organization's core purpose, establishing norms about good performance. As discussed in Chapter 4, purpose matters, and it can be a powerful motivator, helping teams and leaders find meaning in their work. However, a commitment must also be to deliver excellence for that purpose. It is what moves teams from their comfort zone into the performance zone.[117] Leaders who set high-performance standards and create that standard of performance for their teams gain the reputation of being firm but fair. They also push people to be their best while supporting them in that ambition.

Support Operational Autonomy

The best organizations and leaders empower their teams and team members with autonomy to contribute and perform at the highest level possible.[118] They move decisions to the lowest level at which the information is available to make effective decisions. Then, they ensure those individuals have the training, coaching, and freedom to make those decisions and take action effectively.

> **Rather than creating rigid policies for every situation, great leaders establish guiding principles that enable smart decision-making.**

Rather than creating rigid policies for every situation, great leaders establish guiding principles that enable smart decision-making. For example, instead of detailed work-from-home policies that try to account for every scenario, they establish principles about accountability, collaboration, and customer impact that work in any setting. This approach offers flexibility to navigate unique situations while empowering team members to exercise sound judgment. Maintaining alignment with organizational values ensures consistency without unnecessary rigidity. Reducing bureaucracy streamlines decision-making, allowing for greater efficiency and responsiveness. At the same time, it fosters critical thinking across the team, enabling individuals to assess challenges thoughtfully and make informed decisions.

These leaders also ensure that they set the right priorities and systematically eliminate wasted or low-value-added activities for their teams. They provide flexibility, set clear priorities, and optimize time on productive tasks rather than low-value-added meetings. Focusing on principles over policies creates an environment where teams can adapt quickly while staying true to what matters most.

Adopt a Growth Focus

In a growth-focused organization, everyone embraces a mindset in which learning and improvement are valued over "in-the-moment" performance, and strengths are built upon as the foundation of future success.[119] Teams and individuals focused on growth can achieve exponential improvements because they are focused on improvement more than current performance. Learning, and getting better at learning, creates a continuous improvement flywheel building momentum that not only delivers growth, but accelerates it. A growth-focused mindset thrives under leaders who offer actionable feedback, create extraordinary opportunities, and foster an environment of healthy debate and open discourse.

Psychological safety is the most non-negotiable competence for building mutual trust and respect among the above mentioned elements. It enables team members to experiment, take risks, innovate, and simply play together. However, ensuring your team functions at its best goes beyond rote implementation of these elements. It must be (and feel) authentic rather than forced. Finding a way to lighten the atmosphere and deepen the authenticity can be challenging.

One way to tackle this is to consider designing as a bit of fun. Because we often tend to take ourselves too seriously in business, we can inadvertently eliminate the opportunity to play. Look for and create opportunities to have fun and be in the moment. Teams that play together stay together.[120] Friendships between coworkers and kinship amongst the team build loyalty and foster accountability, contributing to better outcomes.

We once had a client who started gaming together on Friday afternoons. The owner confessed that, at first, it felt like a guilty pleasure. But they kept a plethora of productivity numbers. They found that on the weeks when they had scheduled this time to play together on Friday, they had better numbers for the week than when they did not. Some of our best, life-long friends came from bonds forged when playing together on a team or creating shows together. We would do well to look for these kinds of opportunities to forge bonds in our play at work, too. Not only does it make things more fun and interesting, but it also makes for better team relationships.

Creating Your Growth Engine

While mindset forms the foundation, systematic approaches help embed growth into daily operations. Leaders can create structures that reinforce continuous learning and development.[121]

Actionable feedback drives growth when it is specific and focused on behaviors rather than vague observations. It should emphasize future improvement rather than dwelling on past mistakes, ensuring team members can constructively apply it. By tying feedback to its impact, it becomes easier for individuals to understand its significance and relevance. Most importantly, effective feedback should be immediately actionable, providing clear guidance on what can be adjusted or improved immediately. For example, instead of "Your presentations need improvement," actionable feedback might be "When you include specific data points and limit slides to key takeaways, executive audiences can more easily grasp and act on your recommendations."

Creating Development Opportunities Growth happens when challenge meets support.[122] Creating opportunities for growth and development requires a variety of structured experiences that challenge and engage team members. Stretch assignments and cross-functional projects expose individuals to new challenges and perspectives, while innovation initiatives and process improvement encourages creative problem-solving.

Learning partnerships, peer coaching, and mentoring connections foster knowledge-sharing and professional growth. Additionally, knowledge exchanges, skill-building forums, innovation labs, problem-solving workshops, and technical deep dives provide dedicated spaces for continuous learning and skill refinement. These opportunities empower individuals to expand their expertise, collaborate effectively, and drive meaningful contributions within their organization.

Facilitating Healthy Disagreement Growth requires challenging existing assumptions.[123] Create conditions where productive conflict can thrive:

Do:	Don't:
• Establish clear ground rules	• Allow personal attacks
• Focus on issues, not individuals	• Permit passive-aggressive behavior
• Encourage diverse perspectives	• Rush to false consensus
• Drive to action-oriented solutions	• Avoid necessary conflicts

Consider how Adobe transformed its approach to development by replacing traditional performance reviews with regular "check-in" conversations focused on growth and learning. This shift created more frequent opportunities for feedback and development while building stronger manager-employee relationships.[124]

Bringing Together the Foundational Elements of Success: The Tasty Catering Story[125]

These four foundational elements—psychological safety, performance excellence, operational autonomy, and growth focus—create the bedrock for extraordinary team performance. Tasty Catering's transformation illustrates how these elements work together in practice.

Building Psychological Safety

One day, when Tom went to work, he was surrounded by two of his valued team members. He didn't realize it at the time, but he was walking into an intervention. "If you don't change the way you treat us, we are walking," they explained.

At this point, Tom had what he describes as a "wake-up call." He took a good, hard look in the mirror and decided to make some changes. His employees at Tasty Catering helped him understand what they needed, including more psychological safety and greater autonomy.

Driving Performance Excellence

With Tom's support, leadership defined its core values and intentionally integrated them into decision-making, hiring/firing, rewards, and recognition. Tasty Catering set out to transition from a top-down leadership approach to growing a culture of leaders. Tom adopted the mantra that "Management is a job. Leadership is a way of life."

Enabling Operational Autonomy

Tom and his leadership team sought to empower team members to find their own answers. Instead of providing answers, they expected team members to devise three proposed solutions to their questions or problems before Tom would weigh in. This helped team members grow their resourcefulness and recognize their leadership capabilities.

Fostering Growth and Learning

They established a "Good to Great Council" inspired by Jim Collins' book.[126] With team representatives from each department and company ownership, they tackled business challenges with a holistic perspective as they arose. For instance, during the 2008 recession, the team devised the collective decision for shared pay reductions to prevent layoffs. Since the team was given input on the solution, they supported what they created and felt more valued.

The Results of Transformation

Tom was fortunate. When problems arose, his employees felt compelled to speak up and safe enough to share their experiences. They had enough psychological safety and loyalty to the company to voice their concerns, a reality that not every company has. This started a chain reaction of events that led to a company transformation. Tasty Catering not only weathered that storm, but the company and the team came out on the other end, thriving.

Level Up with Kinship and Abundance

While Tasty Catering's story demonstrates the power of these four foundational elements, truly exceptional organizations develop two additional qualities that act as force multipliers - kinship and abundance. These elements transform teams from entities that are the sum of their parts to those that outperform any reasonable expectation. Tasty Catering's success wasn't just about implementing new processes - it was about building deep connections and adopting an abundance mindset that enabled creative solutions even during challenging times.

As we studied different types of organizations, we consistently found them to be the additional differentiators of truly extraordinary teams. Leaders who foster an environment where kinship and abundance can thrive can systematically deliver results surpassing what others believe possible. Furthermore, they create those magical, "I'll never forget this extraordinary team" environments that members remember years later.

Foster Kinship

Kinship fulfills our shared desire for connection, communication, and collaboration.[127] Teams that have developed kinship have a socially constructed experience that taps into a shared purpose, reality,[128] and memories. We experience kinship when our teams become a part of who we are and how we operate. Kinship fuels collaboration on steroids with elements of solidarity and connected motivation.[129] [130] It is often observed in groups of teams who undertake difficult things together and build the kind of bond in which there is an "all for one and one for all" mentality. They have each other's backs.

The most cited examples of this emerge from the crucible experiences in the military, where an intensely loyal "brotherhood" emerges and individuals actively step in and support one another, transferring tasks seamlessly to achieve shared goals. While no business situation can compare to the intensity of battle, there are parallel experiences that mimic many of these themes. We have documented cases of leaders mowing lawns and running errands for developers working around the clock ahead of a product launch, making midnight returns to the office because a colleague needed something urgently, and many more acts of sacrifice in service to their teammates. The combination of loyalty, willingness to support others, and valuing team over individual goals,[131] defines a culture of kinship.

Like strong casts, good teams cover for one another and the unexpected challenges. Years ago, Patrick was in a production of Les Misérables. One of the cast members tore his Achilles tendon during the middle of the run. His understudy stepped in to cover his position, and the rest of the cast shifted to cover the remaining holes in the production. Though they had not been able to rehearse every nuance of the performance, their strong connection to one another and ability to understand and anticipate reactions allowed them to adjust quickly in the moment.

Similarly, there were performances in which an actor dropped a line, missed an entrance cue, or dropped a prop. After the customary split-second alarm, everyone locks in on one another and, with knowing eyes, begins the dance of getting the scene back on track. They could be creative and build upon one another's ideas and energy to deliver a seamless performance. When done well, most of the time, the audience will not know something is off. The same is true for high-performing teams in the workplace. When the team is invested in supporting one another in these respective efforts, you can build off the ideas and the energy that gets created.

You have likely had a similar experience with a team that was so deeply connected that you could compensate for one another and also wanted to lean in and help where you could. When this deep kinship exists, it enables flexibility and the ability to pivot at a moment's notice when the inevitable curveballs come your way.

Adopt an Abundance Mindset to Achieve Resilience

One often overlooked factor in team success is cultivating an attitude of abundance, which ultimately comes down to how situations, choices, and challenges are framed.

Abundance thinking isn't just an individual mindset - it's contagious. Research shows that emotions and attitudes are infectious, spreading naturally throughout organizations.[132] Positive energy, particularly from leaders, can catalyze innovation and resilience across entire teams. This isn't about enforcing toxic positivity or ignoring real challenges - it's about approaching difficulties with a constructive mindset that enables solutions rather than amplifies problems.

In today's AI-driven workplace, abundance thinking becomes even more critical. Rather than viewing AI as a threat, purpose-driven leaders see it as an amplifier of human capability. Organizations that view AI as a tool for amplifying human capability rather than as a threat to replace it are finding new ways to enhance creativity and productivity. This positive energy around technology and change cascades throughout their organizations, affecting adoption and innovation. Leaders who maintain an abundance mindset help their teams see AI and other emerging technologies as tools for augmenting their capabilities rather than replacing them.

Conversely, anxiety and scarcity thinking can create downward spirals that stifle creativity and collaboration.[133] Consider how this plays out in practice. When faced with a challenging deadline, a scarcity-minded leader might say, "We don't have enough time or resources." This triggers stress responses, narrowing thinking, and reducing collaboration. An abundance-minded leader instead asks, "How might we approach this creatively?" This subtle shift opens possibilities and energizes teams.[134]

Three key practices that help embed abundance thinking include reframing constraints, amplifying positive energy, and leveraging collective intelligence.

1. Reframe Constraints

Instead of viewing limitations as barriers, treat them as creative catalysts. One compelling example of the power of constraints is Dr. Seuss. He was challenged to write a book that first graders couldn't put down using less than 225 words - and he delivered "The Cat In the Hat". And when subsequently challenged to create a book with only 50 words, he delivered the classic "Green Eggs and Ham". Similarly, when Pixar faced technical constraints in early animation, they didn't see limitations - they saw opportunities to innovate. This mindset led to breakthrough technologies that transformed the industry.[135] Great teams embrace constraints as an opportunity to innovate and turn bugs into features.

2. Amplify Positive Energy

Leaders play a crucial role in setting the emotional tone for their teams, as their attitudes and behaviors influence the overall work environment. Research indicates that positive emotional contagion fosters improved cooperation, helping teams work harmoniously toward shared goals. It also decreases conflict, creating a more supportive and collaborative atmosphere. Additionally, a positive emotional climate enhances task performance by boosting motivation and focus while encouraging creative problem-solving by fostering a mindset of openness and innovation. By cultivating positivity, leaders can drive both team cohesion and high performance.[136]

3. Leverage Collective Intelligence

AI and new technologies aren't threats in an abundance mindset - they're amplifiers of human capability.[137] Applying these practices helps leaders foster a positive and innovative team culture. Starting meetings by sharing wins and key learnings sets an encouraging tone and reinforces a mindset of progress.

Using "Yes, and..." instead of "Yes, but..." in discussions promotes open collaboration and builds on ideas rather than shutting them down. Celebrating experiments—regardless of their outcome—encourages risk-taking and continuous learning. Framing challenges as opportunities for innovation shifts the focus from obstacles to possibilities. Additionally, creating space for divergent thinking before moving to convergent solutions allows for more creative problem-solving and well-rounded decision-making.

Companies that lack an abundance mindset often approach problems as tradeoffs. They believe they must choose between profit or purpose, quality or volume, growth or efficiency. Instead, if we can lean into the both-and proposition and embrace the organization's strengths and positives, we can unlock its true potential.

When we have a scarcity mindset, we focus on (and often magnify) the costs, limitations, or risks–all the negative factors. We fixate on the risks or perceived losses[138] and overvalue their potential impact.[139] The cognitive bias of loss aversion tends to get us in trouble. As humans, we view the potential of losing (or failing to capture something) more than a potential gain of the same size.

Often, as leaders, we focus on how we failed to get to where we thought we would be and minimize the progress we have made. Worse, we inadvertently establish the norm of focusing on the negative during project reviews, meetings, and when assessing performance. We are not arguing for a Pollyanna approach to leadership, but we are suggesting a better balance. Leaders need to intentionally magnify the value of progress (the gains) to put them on a level playing field with our gaps.

We recommend operating from a mindset of abundance and gratitude. It's essential to recognize that we often set idealized goals above what we can reasonably achieve. Given this, there is great power in assessing yourself not by how much you missed your goals but rather by how far you (or your team) have come from your original baseline.[140] Instead of focusing on that arbitrary vision, focus on what you've gained and how much you've accomplished.

That's embracing an abundance mindset. Positive emotion is contagious, and as leaders, we must be mindful of the energy we exude. Coming from a place of gratitude and possibility-thinking has the power to influence those around us. This mindset creates a resilience that drives sustained high performance.

Another potential method for embracing an abundance mindset is to lean into one element of the Lean or Agile methodology - a Minimum Viable Product (MVP). The principle of an MVP mindset can be applied to anything by giving yourself and your team permission to do something at a "good enough" level intentionally, use it to learn, and then optimize.

We worked with a finance leader who applied this to her transformation initiative. Rather than redesigning the month-end close process and implementing all the new financial systems simultaneously, she created an MVP process. The team learned what worked, refined it, and repeated the process. Over a few short months, they completely transformed their operations. You don't necessarily have to become an Agile or Lean zealot to embrace the value of these methodologies.

With an abundance mindset embedded in a culture of psychological safety, you can encourage experimentation. This will allow your team to build on their strengths and riff off one another's ideas to generate new and innovative ideas. It will also energize your employees and create a virtuous cycle whereby each feeds the other.

To recap, that leaves us with six elements leaders should focus on when developing a purpose-driven culture: Psychological Safety, Performance Excellence, Operational Autonomy, Growth Focus, Kinship, and an Abundance Mindset.

We've provided a detailed framework in Appendix 6A to help you assess how well your current practices support these cultural elements and identify specific improvement opportunities. This tool will help you evaluate your cultural foundation and determine where to focus your enhancement efforts. Use it regularly to ensure your actions and systems consistently reinforce the culture you want to create.

Embed best practices

This may seem like a lot to take in. Still, some practices help you embed these behaviors into your culture as you promote psychological safety, drive performance excellence, provide operational autonomy, embrace a growth focus, develop kinship, and adopt an abundance mindset within your workplace.

1. **Walk the talk.** Model the behaviors you want to create in your company culture. This doesn't happen by accident.

2. **Promote self-awareness and genuine openness to feedback.** When you make a mistake, own it. This doesn't mean self-flagellation. Taking responsibility, allowing grace, and focusing on solving a mistake are essential. Accept feedback without becoming defensive.

3. **Support autonomy and responsibility.** Move decisions and actions to the lowest possible level and encourage their making.

4. **Set high standards.** Establish high but achievable goals that will drive a winning performance. Be clear on your expectations and non-negotiables. Ensure your behavior standards are also well understood. For example, it may be okay to miss a particular goal, but compromising ethical standards is never okay. Model each of these yourself.

5. **Prioritize improvement over performance.** Ensure your reviews and team meetings focus on progress and growth rather than evaluation.

6. **Trade-in blame for curiosity.** Relatedly, don't look to find fault. Ask questions and seek first to understand.

7. **Value the humanity in your team.** Treat your team members with respect and dignity at all times. Instead of the Golden Rule (i.e., do unto others as you would have them do unto you), strive for the Platinum Rule (i.e., do unto others as they want done to them).

8. **Give employees a voice.** Look for ways to include your team members in decision-making whenever possible. Allow them to co-create solutions. We've discussed the importance of this in prior chapters. It's also essential to look for multiple channels for your employees to provide input, to make it easy for them to do so, for different styles and circumstances. Your team has a great deal of wisdom, experience, and creativity to be unlocked, and tapping into it is powerful.

9. **Support constructive conflict, creativity, and innovation.** Instead of ignoring conflict, create healthy ground rules focusing on solutions to issues, not personal attacks. Actively seek out the perspective of others in situations where louder voices may drown out their voices. Demonstrate that it's okay to disagree on issues, provided that it's done respectfully. Encourage brainstorming and looking at things from different angles to support more creative solutions to problems than you might otherwise achieve on auto-pilot.

10. **Support affirmative practices.** Nip negativity in the bud. Again, this does not imply ignoring problems (aka toxic positivity). When someone is not meeting expectations, be clear about the issue and address it by honoring the front rather than the back door (e.g., avoid passive-aggressive comments, humiliation, insensitive humor, or avoidance). Emphasize positive visioning and affirmation of strengths to bring out the best in your team. Strive for the most effective solutions, not necessarily the most efficient ones.

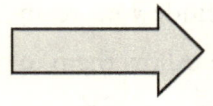 To help you evaluate your leadership approach and identify ways to unlock your team's full potential, we invite you to take our complimentary Leading for Peak Performance Assessment at adlucemgroup.com/additional-resources.

With your culture and community established, it's time to optimize how your team works together. The right systems and processes will amplify your team's effectiveness.

Key Chapter Takeaways

- Create psychological safety.
- Drive performance excellence while fostering a growth mindset.
- Support Operational Autonomy.
- Level up by embracing kinship and abundance.
- Maintain flexibility and awareness that enables you to pivot.
- Maintain and model a spirit of humility and coachability as a leader.

Chapter 6 Reflection Questions

1. What is your sense of the current psychological safety level on your team? What evidence are you basing this on?
2. What barriers exist to genuine collaboration?
3. How can you foster deeper connections among team members?
4. Where do you see opportunities to build more trust?

Chapter 7

Optimize your ways of working

Clarify your focus	Invest in your capabilities	Deliver results
Connect with your purpose	Deepen purpose connection	Be an executive first
Asses the landscape	Upgrade your team	Lead with intention
Craft your vision	Tend to your culture	Architect your role
	Optimize ways of working	Practice agility

"Efficiency is doing things right;
effectiveness is doing the right things."
—Peter Drucker

Simplify, Streamline, Standardize, and Synchronize (4S)

Most organizations have similar access to technology, capabilities, and financials. The challenge isn't about having more time, but rather making thoughtful choices about how we invest the time we have. Ultimately, success boils down to how we use those hours and assets. Leadership is about prioritizing well and setting up an operating system that executes efficiently, a prospect that is much easier said than done. Fortunately, there are a few well-established principles that you can leverage to optimize your ways of working.

Simplify - Less is more

First and foremost, successful organizations prioritize the few high-impact initiatives that will deliver meaningful outcomes rather than spreading efforts thin across too many objectives with marginal results. The best leaders strategically simplify their portfolio and narrow their focus, and that of their organization, to the few, most important things to be undertaken. This flies in the face of our natural inclinations, as most leaders and organizations make the error of believing that doing more will get more. They falsely believe that if four products deliver $4M in revenue, eight projects will deliver $8M. What most technology-based companies have now learned is that more is not more. As Wheelwright & Clark established, less is, in fact, more - that is, starting fewer things results in finishing more.[141]

Consider a section of a 4-lane freeway that supports free-flowing traffic, enabling cars to travel around 55 mph. All works well until rush hour hits, then progress slows to a crawl. Traffic engineers have learned that the counter-intuitive strategy of slowing the flow of cars entering the highways at these times will speed up their commute time. Yep, you heard that right: waiting at those on-ramp lights gets you to your destination faster!

But how?

Ramp lights that meter access to the highways cause minor delays as you get on the highway, prevent slowdowns, lower the risk of accidents, and ultimately maintain steady highway speeds. By strategically choosing not to overtax the system, everything runs at a higher throughput, and more is ultimately accomplished. For traffic, that means more people getting through rush hour traffic faster. For organizations, it means higher output is delivered faster.

Returning to our example of the company expecting to double its productivity by starting 8 projects rather than the 4 it had done in prior years, let's imagine it starts 8 projects. Since it got $4M from those 4 projects in the past, it likely would expect $8M as its ROI on these 8 projects.

Research predicts that such a company will likely only deliver something like $3M - less than they would have delivered by only undertaking 4 projects! Starting more resulted in getting less. And that does not even include the adverse effects of overworking the teams or having staffed people on projects that never come to fruition.

Decades ago, Wheelwright and Clark's groundbreaking research established the connection between focus and operational effectiveness, confirming that focusing on fewer, more strategically impactful initiatives delivers more in the end.[142] In the following years, these same principles were confirmed and used as the underlying principles for Agile. While there are many things that Agile may not get right in its application, the foundational belief that we cannot do more by doing more is both valid and well-substantiated. As the adage says, if one woman can have a baby in 9 months, we can't put 9 women on the job and create a baby in 1 month.

So, the most productive and innovative organizations understand how many simultaneous work streams they can undertake and use that as the target number of initiatives they charter. They know that trying to do more adds complexity, risk, and delays, resulting in being overextended and reducing their output and productivity. They start by understanding their capacity, setting that as their target, and then prioritizing what they will focus on within that limit.

From Principle to Practice: Implementing "Less is More"

While the "less is more" principle sounds straightforward, implementing it requires systematic evaluation and disciplined execution. Many leaders struggle with what to eliminate and how to do so effectively. We propose applying a practical framework, adapted from the Eisenhower Effort-Impact quadrant concept, popularized by Stephen Covey, for identifying what matters most.[143]

To identify and act on what matters most, use this Effort-Impact Matrix to map your activities:

Impact/Effort	Low Effort	High Effort
High Impact	Quick Wins • Easy to implement • Immediate value • Build momentum	Strategic Investments • High value, complex • Resource intensive • Long-term focus
Low Impact	Potential Eliminations • Low value • Low effort • Consider stopping	Immediate Cuts • High effort, low return • Resource drain • Clear elimination candidates

1. Value Analysis: Evaluate Strategic Contribution.

   First, assess each activity's contribution to your strategic goals:

   • Direct Impact: Does this directly advance our key objectives?

   • Indirect Value: Does this enable other high-value activities?

   • Resource Consumption: What is the actual time, money, and energy cost?

- Opportunity Cost: What could we do instead with these resources?

2. Effort-Impact Matrix

Map your activities using this simple but powerful tool:

- High Impact/Low Effort: Your quick wins
- High Impact/High Effort: Your strategic investments
- Low Impact/Low Effort: Your potential eliminations
- Low Impact/High Effort: Your immediate cuts

3. Elimination Criteria

Establish clear decision rules for what to stop doing:

- The "Not Now" Rule: Good ideas that don't serve current priorities
- The "Not Us" Rule: Activities better handled by others
- The "Not Needed" Rule: Legacy activities that no longer add value
- The "Not Working" Rule: Efforts that consistently underperform

4. Implementation Sequence

Create a systematic approach to reduction:

- Start Small: Begin with prominent low-value activities
- Build Momentum: Document and share early wins
- Scale Up: Apply learnings to more complex decisions
- Sustain: Create guards against scope creep

Key Actions:

- High Impact/Low Effort: Prioritize these quick wins
- High Impact/High Effort: Plan and resource strategically

- Low Impact/Low Effort: Evaluate necessity
- Low Impact/High Effort: Eliminate to free-up resources

This simple but powerful tool helps you visualize where to focus your resources. Quick wins in the high-impact, low-effort quadrant should be your priority, while activities in the low-impact, high-effort quadrant are prime candidates for elimination. Strategic investments require careful planning and resourcing, while potential eliminations should be evaluated for necessity.

Consider how one technology executive put this into practice. Faced with dozens of active projects and declining team morale, she implemented this framework with her leadership team. They identified that 40% of their projects consumed an estimated 60% of their resources while contributing less than 20% to their strategic goals. Eliminating these projects freed up innovation capacity and dramatically improved team engagement and delivery speed.

The key is to make this an ongoing practice rather than a one-time exercise. Build in regular checkpoints to assess:

- Are we still focused on what matters most?
- Have new low-value activities crept in?
- Are we saying "no" to the right things?
- Are we maintaining our simplified approach?

Remember, the goal isn't just to do less - it's to create space for what matters most. As you implement this framework, you'll likely find that:

- Decision-making becomes clearer
- Team energy increases
- Innovation flourishes
- Results improve

Simplify - Focus on what matters most

Once they understand their capacity, the best leaders narrow their focus by strategically simplifying their portfolio and competing priorities. As our executive coaching clients often hear our challenge, it's the proverbial "addition by subtraction." Yet, this is much easier said than done.[144] [145] As anyone who has ever tried to downsize knows, dramatically paring down is a hard job, fraught with the risk of choosing the wrong things.

The best approach is to take a step back, use your strategy as the benchmark, and ask yourself, "If I were going to deliver on my strategy, what few key things must I do?" That simple question should help you determine what is core to your future. Those become your Strategic Initiatives.[146]

Then, take a hard look at the other things you wanted to accomplish (likely, they are cemented in your mind or your organization's mind as "have to do" items). Ask yourself the following questions to determine the best path forward. The key in this process is to look for the FIRST TIME you can say no and act on that to eliminate as much as possible.

- **Do we have to do it AT ALL?** - What if we didn't do it at all? What would be the consequences? Do we even need to do it if it does not have a high impact?
- **Do we have to do it NOW?** - What if we delayed it and did it later? Could we gain something by waiting until we have more information?
- **Do we have to do ALL OF IT?** What if we didn't do everything? Is there a way to do only the most critical part of it? Is there a way to do a lighter-weight version of it? Can we

separate it into multiple things, keeping what we must do but eliminating the rest?

- **Do we have to do it THIS WAY?** Is there a different way to do this that would take less effort, less time, or consume fewer of our most critical resources?
- **Do we have to do it THIS WELL?** Can we capture the benefits we need by using a good enough approach? Can we put lower-skilled, less critical labor on it?
- **Do we have to do it FOREVER?** Can we phase it out? Even if we can't say no now, can we say no later and build that into the plan?

Remember, simplifying aims to move your business ahead and deliver on the most critical parts of your strategy. But it's not just about organizational success - simplification is equally essential for your effectiveness and career trajectory. The ability to cut through complexity and focus on what truly matters is increasingly recognized as a hallmark of executive excellence. Leaders who master this skill not only deliver better business results but also experience less burnout, make better decisions, and build stronger reputations as strategic thinkers.

It may be hard to "let go" of the other things you have "always done." Still, it serves a greater purpose - eliminating the chaos and noise that gets in the way of organizational performance and your leadership impact. It is the first step in designing and leading for efficiency. Seize the opportunity to create a new working environment that sets you and your organization up for success. Simplifying allows you and your team to focus on what matters most and minimize the distractions and overhead that get in the way of doing so.

Streamline

Optimize your processes to be as efficient as possible as you deliver on your simplified list of focus areas. Organizations that are good at streamlining are dedicated to learning from best and worst practices; they pull in learnings and incorporate them into their working methods. They actively look at how they have accomplished things in the past and look specifically for both what went well and what went poorly.[147]

Most process improvement approaches are built upon giants like Frank and Lillian Gilbreth[148] whose motion studies and research (not to mention their experience raising 12 children) gave us new ways to optimize how we work. Many approaches to improving and streamlining work have since been developed and used, including Is / Should Mapping, Lean Six Sigma, Business Process Improvement, Root Cause Analysis, Continuous Process Improvement, and Kaizen, just to name a few. We have leveraged many of them throughout our careers, and any of these techniques can help you streamline your work. What matters most is that it works for your organization and that you adhere to key streamlining principles.

We have worked with hundreds of companies that vary significantly by industry, workforce, size, dominant function, culture, country, and growth rate. One constant for all of them is that change is always a challenge. If you are trying to change your workflows or processes, it is best to do that with a familiar approach as much as possible. It minimizes the resistance you will get as you try to change the process. If you work somewhere Kaizen is used, lean into that to make these changes. Similarly, leverage a retrospective to discuss process improvements if you are a Lean or Agile shop. We often use Is / Should Mapping (there's a basic description in Appendix 7A and a list of resources if you need a framework from which to start) with elements of Appreciative Inquiry. Still, whatever method you use, the most important thing is to focus on the underlying principles you adhere to.

Organizations that effectively streamline their processes typically adhere to the same set of principles no matter what approach they use:

- **Identify problems.** Focus on the problems (roadblocks, disconnects, delays, and barriers) and figure out how to eliminate or solve them.
- **Eschew blame.** They focus on fixing the system rather than determining who or what is to blame for a problem.
- **Close performance gaps.** They look for dips in performance, find the root causes, and find ways to address them.
- **Keep what's working.** Rather than focusing solely on what's broken or wrong, they focus on what's working well and double down on it.
- **Embrace possibilities.** They aim high, going beyond closing performance gaps and fixing errors, and ask themselves what "could be true" or what "might be possible" if we were at our very best.
- **Employ diverse perspectives.** They add outsiders and those with different experiences. It's hard to see and create new solutions if you come from the same point of view.
- **Create buy-in.** They engage a broad group of stakeholders to co-create the new streamlined process. This ensures a better solution and better buy-in across the organization.

Standardize

Most leaders and teams find that most of their day is consumed by low-value-added tasks that eat away at the hours available for taking on strategic, essential, and high-value-added tasks. Some of these are called keeping the lights on (KTLO) tasks, such as monthly reporting, maintenance, audits, payroll, etc. Often, it feels like a reality we simply can't escape. However, the most effective leaders standardize as many tasks as possible. Standardizing is about having a good, hard look at your team's tasks, determining best practices, and automating everything they can.

When looking to standardize, consider the following best practices.[149] [150]

- **Modularize.** Break down repetitive work into standard task sets. Often, these will cut across several processes.
- **Identify best practices.** This is where you can re-apply the process improvement approaches at a lower / task level. Look for examples of when these tasks were completed faster or more easily and replicate those approaches.
- **Eliminate Non-Value-Added Steps:** Remove steps that do not contribute to the desired outcome or customer value.
- **Automate and Use Technology:** Use standardized tools and software to automate routine or repetitive tasks (e.g., workflow automation software, robotic process automation (RPA), and AI-powered solutions). Integrate digital tools (e.g., project management platforms, customer relationship management systems, accounting systems) to streamline communication, tracking, and reporting.
- **Codify and Communicate.** Outline the ideal steps for performing a task, making the process as transparent as possible.

The easier it is for the whole organization to understand what is happening, the more likely it is to execute and improve continuously.

Synchronize

The most often overlooked component for optimizing work is considering how you sequence and schedule work in your group and with other parts of the organization. Steven Spear and his colleagues at MIT view synchronization as a vital step in not only delivering efficiencies in performance but also in creating a system that enables ongoing improvements.[151][152] Integrated workflows are meant to be seamless and ensure all stakeholders understand how their work impacts the broader system and how the broader system impacts their work.

The key principle to adhere to when synchronizing work is to ensure that handoffs are planned to eliminate inefficiencies, particularly when coordinating tasks between teams, departments, or divisions. Consistent protocols and formats for transferring information or work can help ensure errors are minimized. In addition, consider triggers (or automated alerts or signals) that alert everyone when disconnects or delays happen. The goal is not to make the processes rigid but rather to allow them to be transparent and progress to be observable. That makes monitoring and improving them easier, ultimately making them more adaptive and resilient.

When considering the rhythms and routines of your team, we encourage you to map out what needs to happen daily, weekly, monthly, quarterly, and annually, and what goal each activity delivers. A best practice is to capture it in a shareable form (example provided in Appendix 7B) and share it with your team and the organization. It is a compelling way to establish clarity and fuel improved cross-functional collaboration. It also provides a foundation for working together to challenge how things are being done and identify potential improvement opportunities.

Part of synchronization is ensuring feedback loops are embedded into every part of the process. Synchronization is not static; it must evolve with the business and improve with learning. Whenever possible, immediate triggers or feedback are the best, but the priority here is that it is always easy for everyone to see deviations, bottlenecks, errors, and opportunities for improvement. In addition, every process should include controlled ways to experiment and improve that don't disrupt the system.

For example, one tech company we worked with designated week three every month for changing financial and infrastructure processes and systems. Everyone knew when it would happen, and it was strategically scheduled after the month-end close and before the sales push at the end of the month. It worked brilliantly and enabled continuous improvement to systems that were otherwise hard to change.

Synchronizing processes focus on real-time coordination, feedback loops, goal alignment, and continuous improvement. By embedding these principles into workflows, organizations can achieve seamless operations, adaptability, and sustained high performance.

Build a Learning Organization

The hallmark of efficient systems is that they adhere to all four S's outlined above and are designed to empower joint ownership and learning. Leaders should foster a mindset of shared responsibility, curiosity, and continuous improvement, where teams collaborate to identify and improve the business. Silos and finger-pointing have no place in high-velocity organizations, as knowledge-sharing and cross-pollination are required for sustainable performance.[153] Learning organizations that consistently look for ways to understand and improve, systematically look for ways to communicate system-wide, and feed it into their decision-making processes consistently outperform their peers.[154] [155] [156] [157]

One of the key enablers of both team and organizational success is the ability to learn from mistakes, improve on past efforts, and challenge the status quo. Time and again, research has demonstrated the connection between learning and sustained high performance.[158] [159] [160] High-performing teams treat errors and failures as opportunities for learning and improvement,[161] and rather than punishing failures, they promote innovators because they prioritize long-term improvements.[162]

However, achieving such a system requires building robust systems that drive continuous improvement, innovation, and adaptability[163] and maintaining a culture of collaboration and psychological safety[164] that supports it. Central to this learning system is the practice of actionable feedback.

Actionable Feedback Framework

While many organizations understand the importance of feedback, truly actionable feedback has specific characteristics that drive improvement:

- Specific and behavioral: Focus on observable actions rather than personality traits
- Future-focused: Emphasize what can be done differently next time rather than dwelling on past mistakes

- Tied to impact: Connect behaviors to business outcomes and team effectiveness
- Immediately actionable: Provide clear, concrete steps for improvement

For example, instead of "You need to communicate better," actionable feedback might be "When you provide weekly updates that include progress and obstacles, the team can collaborate more effectively to solve problems." This approach enhances the effectiveness of feedback by making it more objective, minimizing bias, and focusing on facts rather than opinions. Reducing defensive reactions fosters a more open and constructive dialogue, allowing individuals to engage with feedback productively. It also provides a clear path to improvement, ensuring that feedback leads to actionable steps rather than uncertainty. Additionally, this method strengthens problem-solving capabilities and promotes continuous learning within the team, creating a culture of growth and development.

Leaders who consistently provide and encourage this type of feedback create an environment where continuous improvement becomes natural and expected. The challenge as a leader is to bring such a system to life.[165] [166]

Structure Learning for Sustainable Impact

While effective feedback creates the foundation for improvement, sustainable organizational learning requires systematic knowledge-sharing and development approaches. Some essential elements of high-velocity learning have already been discussed in each aspect of the 4-Ss we covered earlier. However, these can be expanded by enabling knowledge sharing, experimentation, collaboration, and innovation opportunities. A best practice is creating forums where opportunities for improvement are served up, and multiple perspectives on how they might be addressed can be gathered. These typically include:

- **Problem-Solving Workshops:** Cross-functional teams tackle specific challenges, focusing on root cause analysis and generating implementable solutions while building collaborative problem-solving skills

- **Innovation Forums:** Regular sessions that mix structured and informal formats to share new ideas, encourage experimentation, and build on collective insights

- **Knowledge-Sharing Channels:** Digital platforms and processes that make expertise accessible, document lessons learned, and enable organic collaboration

- **Learning Reviews**: Regular reflection on successes and failures that focus on improvement rather than blame, capturing actionable insights to share broadly across the organization

LEARNING IN PRACTICE

Successful organizations create multiple forums for knowledge sharing and improvement, e.g.:

- **Problem-Solving Workshops**
  Cross-functional teams tackle specific challenges
  Focus on root cause analysis
  Generate implementable solutions
  Build collaborative problem-solving skills

- **Innovation Forums**

  Regular sessions to share new ideas

  Mix of structured and informal formats

  Encourage experimentation

  Build on others' insights

- **Knowledge-Sharing Channels**

  Digital platforms for real-time sharing

  Document lessons learned

  Make expertise accessible

  Enable organic collaboration

- **Learning Reviews**

  Regular reflection on successes/failures

  Focus on improvement not blame

  Capture actionable insights

  Share broadly across organization

The ultimate goal of learning is to enable adaptability and resilience, which requires the ability to experiment. A trial and error method, testing minor changes, and then piloting the results is the best approach as it minimizes the risk while not shutting down innovation.[167] Paired with solid performance data and anchored to the organization's goals, it empowers future-focused improvements that create sustainable competitive advantage even in the most challenging environments. But achieving this requires a level of transparency and cross-functional collaboration that requires leaders to operate as a team, managing conflicts and tearing down functional silos.

> **The ultimate goal of learning is to enable adaptability and resilience, and this requires the ability to experiment. Taking pilot approaches can minimize risk while encouraging innovation.**

The environment required to support this learning also requires leaders to cultivate a culture of psychological safety. This not only means making it safe to call out mistakes but also one in which ideas can be shared across all levels and functions. Information flow must be free and open for learning to happen. Open dialogue and constructive feedback must be the norm. Making it a part of the culture requires more of leaders than anyone else, as they regularly model receiving constructive feedback, calling out their own mistakes, and actively encouraging and rewarding others for voicing their ideas and opinions. The good news is that leaders who create a learning environment have teams that more proactively and effectively address challenges.

Now that we've built the framework for success in this section, let's focus on delivery in the next section. This starts with understanding your role as an executive first, beyond your functional expertise.

Key Chapter Takeaways

- Less is more - focus on fewer, more impactful initiatives.
- Push through performance plateaus systematically with the 4Ss (simplify, streamline, standardize, and synchronize).
- Break large goals into smaller achievable steps.
- Build a learning organization to enable continuous improvement.

Chapter 7 Reflection Questions

1. What activities consume time but add little value?
2. How could you simplify complex processes?
3. Where are your team's current performance plateaus?
4. What systems could help sustain continuous improvement?

PART III

Deliver Results

With your framework in place—a purpose-driven team, strong culture, and optimized operations—we turn to delivering results. These final chapters help you bring everything together to achieve sustained high performance.

Chapter 8

Be an Executive First

Clarify your focus	Invest in your capabilities	Deliver results
Connect with your purpose	Deepen purpose connection	**Be an executive first**
Asses the landscape	Upgrade your team	Lead with intention
Craft your vision	Tend to your culture	Architect your role
	Optimize ways of working	Practice agility

"What got you here won't get you there"[168]
—Marshall Goldsmith

You must think and operate beyond your department and priorities to be effective. Too many leaders make the mistake of thinking their primary (and most challenging) role is to deliver on their goals and lead their function. And frankly, that is precisely what success in their careers to date has taught them. Unfortunately, scores of great functional leaders never stepped up to be executives and, as a result, had their careers cut short. Don't fall into that trap.[169]

That was the mistake several of those we have worked with have made, including John, an executive at a software company. John is brilliant and hardworking, and he consistently laid down years of incredible business performance that had him skyrocketing through the ranks. When chosen for the C-suite, he had a clear formula for success - ruthlessly focusing on the one or two most important things needing transformation, eliminating all other distractions, and quickly demonstrating results. His laser-like focus had consistently earned him accolades, and in his new, higher-stress world, he was leaning into this proven formula.

Yet, while that works well for managers and project leaders, it can be the kiss of death for executives. It nearly cost John his job. Leaders at this level must not only deliver results within their span of control against today's objectives but also think about the broader organization's needs and anticipate future needs. Unfortunately, prior roles rarely prepare leaders for this shift, and it is all too typical for a new executive to stumble. Bill, the executive we referenced earlier, also fell into that same trap - and now coaches every one of his new executives on navigating it better than he did.

Leaders must not only attend to today's priorities and crises but also anticipate and prevent tomorrow's challenges.[170] It is one of the key contributing factors to the downfall of many successful companies. They find themselves disrupted due to new entrants, competitive threats, or market shifts that they never saw coming.[171] It is also a contributing factor for leaders who ultimately fail,[172] particularly beyond their first few years.[173] Getting off to a great start by fixing the current problem or a single functional component is a great start. Unfortunately, it's like focusing on getting out to a good start with a great offensive play, only to find that you lose the game because you have no defense and your existing offensive plan has been played out.

As a C-level executive (and frankly at each increasingly higher level of the organization), a leader's job is to monitor a broader landscape, ensuring that today's challenges and priorities are addressed and future challenges and opportunities are anticipated. Those may not be in your functional area or even the current part of the business that is currently the priority. Step out of your role as an operator or a leader of your function and think about the business's long-term success. But a word of caution: this will require proactive leadership and a cross-functional mindset.

Broaden your view

First and foremost, we encourage you to look at the big picture. Take a genuinely strategic mindset and understand the challenges and opportunities for the organization. Research has established that effective leaders are also effective strategists,[174] [175] but doing so requires that they pay attention to more than just the functions they lead. They must keep their eyes on the horizon, understand the market dynamics and shifts, and challenge their peers to do the same. Fighting the tendency to become myopic and instead maintaining a strong network outside your function, your company, and your industry is strongly linked to the long-term success of both executives and their companies.[176]

Kelley, a strategic thought leader in the financial services space, described the challenge of strategy as the ability to "see around corners," enabling you to anticipate what your business would need to deal with in the future. We believe there is no better description of the strategic responsibility of executives. All too often, leaders reflect on their current situation and their own department's operational metrics to confirm what they should focus on. They look for drops in revenue, shifts in their customer base, and parts of their functions that are less efficient or less profitable than they should be. All of the things their careers so far have taught them to pay attention to.

Instead, look externally, around those corners, and thoroughly assess what will set the organization up for long-term success, what will get in the way of that (and therefore needs to be addressed), and how you can contribute to its success. Yes, your function and your functional expertise will likely have a role in that, but the company needs more from you; they need your ability to look around corners to identify opportunities and shape how you will collectively, as a company, face the upcoming challenges.

Of course, there are hundreds of primers, frameworks, and approaches to strategy development and leadership, including tried and true approaches from the leading business schools and consulting firms.[177] [178] [179] But rather than taking a deep dive into how to craft optimal strategy, which would be a book in and of itself, we are going to suggest that you do what few leaders do: Rise above the mechanics, reground yourself on the organization's purpose, and ask (and answer) the underlying question, "How will we win?"

We are not suggesting that strategy frameworks are not useful - they are. But they are ultimately inputs into your evaluation of what is. They will be critical to your organization now and in the future for delivering its purpose, determining what could get in the way, and determining what you must do to ensure your long-term success.

Below are some key questions we recommend as you pressure test your strategy. Good answers are short and precise and often involve only one or two things. If you are creating a long list, take the time to narrow it down to what's really at the core of it and the one or two things that will be at the heart of your success.

- **What is truly special about our business?** What is our value proposition? What do we offer our customers? Ideally, this is something that no one else can replicate.
- **What do our customers want?** Is it changing and evolving? What are our competitors giving them, and how does it compare to our offer?
- **What is our theory of success?** What is our approach to winning in the market? How is it working, and does it need to change? Will it need to change in the future based on market trends? What is our ideal future approach to the business?
- **If we were at our very best, what would be true?** Is it something about our products, our systems, or our prices? What few things must we focus on to get there? How far are we from that today?
- **If our competitors were going to beat us, how would they?** What are the most likely scenarios? What capabilities, resources, or market opportunities set them up to be able to do it?
- **What would keep us from winning?** What risks, roadblocks, or obstacles would bring us down?

Make Peers Your First Team

"Business Moves at the Speed of Relationships"
—Todd Herman

Unfortunately, sales problems often begin with decisions made in product months or years earlier. Manufacturing issues emerge based on capital allocation choices by finance or design decisions by product or projections from marketing. The root causes of today's challenges are not just in the past but often originated in other functions and areas of the organization. Anticipating and combating these strategic challenges requires executives to be both forward-thinking and cross-functional in their approach.

Successful executives work cross-functionally, building relationships across the organization, understanding the strategic and competitive landscape, and establishing a shared agenda with their peers that aligns with the organization's strategy.[180] [181] MIT's Patrick Winston, famous for his *How to Speak* lecture, famously cited the critical factors for success as thought leadership (which he referred to as the quality of your ideas) and the ability to communicate with others effectively.[182] Success at the executive level requires that you leverage these capabilities in three critical focus areas: developing strong peer relationships, a strategic point of view of the business, and the skills to navigate political challenges.[183]

Great executives recognize their peer group as their primary team, or what some call their "first team." [184] [185] [186] [187] As a middle manager, you have the luxury of maintaining a narrow focus centered on the part of the organization that works for you. Once you become an executive, this is no longer the case. A significant part of your role is to understand what is going on in the organization, and there is no better way to ensure that is happening than to develop solid working relationships with your peers.[188]

One Chief Product Officer we worked with established a systematic peer relationship-building approach in her first 90 days. She scheduled monthly one-on-ones with each peer executive, rotating the focus between their priorities, shared challenges, and potential collaborations. During a significant platform migration, this investment paid dividends - when technical issues threatened to impact sales targets, her strong relationship with the Chief Revenue Officer enabled them to quickly develop a joint mitigation strategy that protected both customer experience and revenue goals. This kind of peer partnership doesn't happen accidentally - it requires intentional cultivation and maintenance.

Building trust will ensure that you can surface potential issues early, anticipate where potential problems could arise, and seek win-win solutions.[189] Understanding what is happening in their part of the company and their priorities, as well as becoming partners, sets you and your team up for success.

While this may make many new executives feel disloyal to or unsupportive of their teams, it enables them to support those working under you much more effectively. At one point or another, we all have had the frustration of working for a manager who was constantly surprised and couldn't see shifts in priorities and the organization coming. When that's the case, the entire team is regularly whipsawed from one thing to another, never knowing what will change next and feeling as if their voices aren't heard at an organizational level. When the leader is surprised, the whole team is surprised, and few surprises (other than birthday surprises) are ever good.

Building these "first team" relationships has the added benefit of helping you develop a strategic perspective on the organization and a powerful point of view on how your department and team will support that. Good leaders keep their eyes on the horizon in search of challenges and changes, understand the organization's strategy, and have a voice in shaping and shifting it where necessary.

Strategy is about finding powerful ways to consistently leverage the organizational capabilities to deliver what your customers need better than anyone else. You must know enough about your market, customers, and capabilities to contribute a unique point of view to setting the strategy and associated priorities across the organization. Your role is helping to shape and set priorities so they can be executed effectively. Your job is to consider what will best serve your organization's customers and deliver on your strategic agenda.

This deep connection to your peers and an organization-spanning network will help you navigate the organization's political landscape. Inevitably, conflict will arise, and the ability to orchestrate a solution sets great leaders apart. Strong working relationships and a solid understanding of the strategy and priorities help executives traverse the political landscape. But that's just the beginning.

You must consider your area's role in the organization's overall value chain. Consider how you serve your customers and stakeholders. How do others integrate with that? How can you align all of your objectives? Once you understand what an optimal solution would be, how will you leverage your network and understanding of the strategic context to influence key stakeholders? You are ultimately using your influence to negotiate for what's best for the organization.

But this great perspective is only as good as your ability to communicate, coordinate, and execute. Doing that requires a focused leadership agenda, relationship strategy, and communication plan. You need to develop a working rhythm and style that works for you, that feels effortless and well-balanced. Whether you call that flow, mojo, or having a good groove going, it's ultimately about creating a way of working that allows you to deliver your absolute best as effortlessly as possible. While that sounds easy, it's not, and sometimes you need a little help.

Plan Key Touchpoints

"Your greatest danger is letting the urgent things crowd out the important."[190] —Charles E. Hummel

Nothing meaningful happens by accident. With so much work that needs to get done and an ever-changing list of priorities, it can be easy to sacrifice building and maintaining good connections. Honestly, who hasn't begun a new year or role with all the best intentions, only to have one crisis after another whittle away at the plan until there's nothing left of it in your calendar? To combat this, be intentional about nurturing your internal and external relationships and create a plan that's easy to update and track.

One of the best approaches to this we have seen in play comes from Mary, an executive who consistently sets the standard for nurturing and growing her network at every level of the organization. She has been successful in every role she has taken, and one key contributing factor has been how intentional she is about staying focused on building and maintaining key relationships.

At the beginning of each year, or when starting a new role, she gets out her Excel spreadsheet (we have termed it the "Mary Matrix") and maps all individuals inside and outside the organization that she needs to work with and nurture relationships with, determines the frequency for each interaction, and then schedules them for the whole year. Doing it at the beginning of each year and then checking in with it every quarter is a great way to master staying well-connected in the organization and on top of what matters most. It also sets her up to slay in every job she's had. An example is provided in Appendix 8A.

Get a Battle Buddy

WOODY:	Has everyone picked a moving buddy?
HAMM:	Moving buddy?! You can't be serious!
REX:	Well, I didn't know we were supposed to have one already.
MR. POTATO HEAD:	Do we have to hold hands?
WOODY:	Oh, yeah, you guys think this is a big joke. We've only got one week left before the move. I don't want any toys left behind. **A moving buddy—if you don't have one, get one!**[191] —*Toy Story, 1995*

Too many of us think we should be able to handle everything on our own, but that's our hubris talking. In reality, nothing great was ever accomplished alone; everyone needs someone to watch their blind spots. Craig, a former Coast Guard officer, USAA Chief Strategy Officer, and current CTO for the City of San Antonio, espouses the value of having a Battle Buddy. This is a long-established military practice of assigning servicemembers as buddies to support one another on the battlefield (and often beyond).[192] [193] This is someone who has your back, can provide help when you need it, and is the person for whom you would do the same.

So, as you step into this role, find a battle buddy, a peer who wants you to succeed, who will be a good sounding board, can tell you when you are about to step into it, and sees the world slightly differently than you. But choosing wisely is just the beginning; listen to them with an open mind, and do whatever you can to ensure they are comfortable sharing the hard truths you need to hear if required. Nurture this relationship and ensure that they get this same kind of support from you because a great Battle Buddy is an excellent investment in your long-term success.

We have had the privilege of ringside seats to quite a few executive transitions, and a key contributor to successful ones is how they embrace being an executive first. Bill, whose story we discussed in earlier chapters, estimates that 60+% of his focus is on the company executive role because "only I can do this, and if I don't do it, then my team suffers." His experience and opinions are confirmed by research, and the approaches we shared are techniques used by those who ultimately thrive in those roles.

Your executive perspective provides the context needed to lead your team effectively. Let's explore how to translate this broader view into concrete team leadership.

Key Chapter Takeaways

- Make your peers your first team.
- Think and operate beyond your department or function.

- Broaden your point of view to think strategically.
- Plan key touchpoints intentionally to support your internal and external network.
- Think broadly: Set priorities based on the organization, not your function.
- Get a battle buddy for support.

Chapter 8 Reflection Questions

1. How effectively are you operating at an executive level?
2. What relationships need more investment?
3. How well do you balance functional and organizational responsibilities?
4. Where might you need to delegate more?

Chapter 9

Lead Your Team with Intention

Clarify your focus	Invest in your capabilities	Deliver results
Connect with your purpose	Deepen purpose connection	Be an executive first
Asses the landscape	Upgrade your team	**Lead with intention**
Craft your vision	Tend to your culture	Architect your role
	Optimize ways of working	Practice agility

"If you want to build a ship, don't drum up people to collect wood and don't assign them tasks and work, but rather teach them to long for the endless immensity of the sea."
—Antoine de Saint-Exupéry

Align Up and Out

When we think about setting leaders up for success, the first step is to ensure that their work is integral to and aligned with the business's most important strategic challenges. Your team needs you to provide a critical leadership role, navigating the political landscape on their behalf, taking in the big picture of the organizational and strategic landscape, making appropriate tradeoffs, and setting the right priorities.

In short, they need you to play a more significant role at the organizational level for them to succeed. They need you to set the appropriate agenda and run the interference that they can't run for themselves. If they are the offensive team, you are the coach, quarterback, and the defense all rolled into one. Doing so requires you to invest your time in playing well at the organizational level.

Chapter 3 discussed clarifying your mandate and fleshing out your vision. Building on that foundation, you will want to ensure that it aligns with the rest of the organizational goals and priorities and supports them in a foundational way. This is when you want to ensure your leadership is on board with your plans and approach.

Second, you will need to check in and build alignment with your peers, ensuring that your work won't hit speed bumps or roadblocks when it's time to execute because it isn't well matched to other priorities across the business. Your BHAG, to propel your success, should not only excite and energize your leadership but also do the same for your peers across the organization.

Once your leadership and peers are aligned and you have widespread organizational support, it's time to engage and energize your team.

Energize and enable your team

Of the leadership skills you need, your team is most dependent upon your ability to build a foundation for integrating their collective knowledge, navigate tradeoffs, see the big picture, and set the appropriate agenda.[194] In the prior chapter, we discussed how to set yourself up to have the context and strong connections to do this. But it's not just your knowledge and connections they need from you. They need your energy.

Your attitude and approach have an outsized ability to shape the way your team operates, and research shows that the best leadership style combines positive energy[195] [196] and leadership humility.[197] [198] Research conducted by Kim Cameron and further developed by an entire cadre of scholars has confirmed the strong connection between extraordinary results and a focus on strengths rather than just weaknesses and problems.[199] When you consider it, it makes perfect sense.

Let's say you are running a garage responsible for car repairs. If you only study the repairs that customers were unhappy with, you would learn (and could fix) all the problems that caused complaints. In the best case, you can eliminate all the negatives and bring your bad experiences up to the average. By contrast, if you instead focused on what caused customers to be pleased with their experiences, you might learn things you could use to improve everyone's experiences and raise the overall average experience.

It can be all too tempting to focus on problems that merely need fixing, but leaders who lean into the positive rather than negative are better able to help their teams leverage their strengths to power success.[200] [201] [202]

One additional thought on this topic is that today's hybrid and virtual workplaces make this even more challenging. We must find ways to support our teams well across various working environments. Leaders must bridge physical distances while maintaining personal connections. This means being deliberately transparent about challenges, consciously creating space for authentic dialogue, and finding new ways to make virtual interactions meaningful.

This positive energy is even more powerful when combined with leader humility. Amy Edmondson's work around high-performing teams has established the need for leaders to demonstrate situational humility to lay the foundation for team engagement.[203] [204] Humble leaders, per Collins in *Good to Great*[205] and *Level 5 Leaders,*[206] understand and openly acknowledge their limitations and view them not as liabilities, but merely as realities. They don't assume they are the most intelligent person in the room. They actively defer to others with more expertise when appropriate. In addition, they engage their network and ask for help and outside input.

Research from Harvard Business School and beyond supports the power of being well-networked and leveraging its breadth and diversity to help expand and deepen your knowledge base.[207] [208] [209] Furthermore, we have observed, for two decades, through our relationships with Collaborative Gain's Executive Councils, the transformative power of asking for help. The conclusion is clear: humble leaders who ask for help outperform their peers as individuals and establish behavioral patterns that enable greater success for their teams.

This combination of positive energy and leadership humility creates the foundation for effective team leadership. When you model these qualities, you enhance your effectiveness and establish the conditions for your team to thrive. With this mindset, you can focus on what truly matters most—defining clear direction and expectations for your team.

Focus on What Matters Most

Now that you have considered your role as an executive, it's time to consider your role as a team leader. Onboard and set up your team in a way that ensures that they are not only aligned with your organization's mission but also set up to succeed. As a team leader, you must establish a relatable, inspiring, and attainable vision. If you miss the mark in this, your team will be unable to see themselves and their role. A simple framework you can use for this is:

We help (insert customer) to (whatever need you meet) so that (whatever desired results they can achieve).

You needn't follow this formula exactly, as numerous variations on this theme and plenty of good resources go deeper into this topic (you can search magnetic messaging). However, it is imperative to be succinct and clear in every conversation so they know your mission.

1. Be clear on who you serve
2. The problem you solve
3. And what makes you the greatest at it

Second, you will need to clarify what good looks like. You must have the same level of clarity for this as you do for your mission.

1. Be clear on your goals (your overarching BHAG)
2. How you will achieve them (your approach)
3. And how you will measure success (a specific, time-bound, measurable target)

Keep this message front and center in communications with your team so they know their future mission and goals. Doing so will ensure that you and your team are consistently aligned and that they can prioritize delivering on your most important goals.

This brings us to two fundamental elements of team success: defining the "what" - the clear objectives your team must achieve, and the "how" - how they'll work together to achieve them. Let's examine each of these elements in turn.

Define "What" Your Team Should Do

Ultimately, your team should be focused on fulfilling its mission with excellence.

Get Clear on Your Mission

Your team's purpose should be a clear vision to drive you and your team forward. It will act as your true north and shared reason for showing up every day and giving it your all. It must articulate the unique value you deliver to your customers and how your team supports that.

While it should be connected to and supportive of the organization's purpose, it should articulate its unique role. This connection to purpose has been a well-established contributor to organizations that outperform the market and their peer groups, whether startups or Fortune-500, public or private, small or multinational.[210] [211] Furthermore, a strong connection to purpose and mission improves the connection to meaning for individual staff members and performance.

Commit to Excellence

A clear mission is not sufficient to achieve greatness. Instead, it must be backed by a commitment to excellence in performance, a concept we discussed in Chapter 6 as a key element of your culture. Let's think back to the Miracle on Ice US Olympic Hockey Team, their shared purpose of capturing gold, and their unwavering commitment to putting in the hard work of delivering on that vision.

Being purpose-driven helps ensure directional alignment. A commitment to excellence helps ensure that you and your team are doing what matters most to get there and are aiming for nothing less than your best. This consistent focus on excellence has, not surprisingly, been shown to be a performance differentiator.[212] It makes the difference between a team that is satisfied with mediocre and one that is striving to continuously put forward their absolute best and strive to improve continuously. High standards for and expectations around performance establish a strong benchmark against which progress toward your goals can be measured.

The most potent tools to leverage here are good, focused KPIs. When you are thinking of KPIs, the best advice we can give is that they should be like the US Marines, whose slogan is:

The Few. The Proud. The Marines.[213]

Your KPIs should also be the few and the proud:

- The Few - no more than you can count on one hand.
- The Proud - clear stand-out performance measures, without question about their quality, validity, or relevance.

Define "How" Your Team Should Do It

Build Culture with Intention

As discussed in Chapter 6, the culture you establish is one of the most powerful ways to impact your team and your organization. Like the air we breathe, while largely invisible, it profoundly affects how we show up and perform. The best leaders build a culture that supports a One Team/One Mission mentality, actively embraces mistakes, shares credit, and communicates transparently and authentically.[214] This culture creates the psychological safety we explored earlier, enabling innovation and continuous improvement while fostering the kinship that drives extraordinary performance.

Leaders should model behavior consistent with this culture and create systems and programs that reinforce and support these behaviors across their teams. This might include:

- Starting meetings by celebrating learning from mistakes
- Creating forums where teams can safely experiment with new approaches
- Establishing regular cross-functional collaboration opportunities
- Implementing recognition programs that reward team success over individual achievement
- Building feedback mechanisms that encourage open dialogue
- Designing decision-making processes that value diverse perspectives

Remember that culture is built one decision, interaction, and moment at a time. Every policy you implement, meeting you run, or feedback you provide either reinforces or undermines your desired culture. As research from Harvard Business School and beyond has consistently demonstrated, cultures like this not only support higher performance but create sustainable competitive advantage through increased innovation, engagement, and retention.[215] [216] [217] [218]

The key is consistency between what you say matters and what you actually reinforce through your actions and systems. For instance, if you say innovation matters but punish failed experiments, your real culture will quickly become risk-averse regardless of your stated values. Similarly, if you promote collaboration but reward individual achievement, you'll create internal competition rather than the kinship and abundance mindset we discussed in Chapter 6.

Create Your High-Performance Community

While culture sets the context for your team and how they should behave, their ability to create a community, working collectively, will impact whether they become more or less than the sum of their parts. In a community, the team supports one another and is, in turn, supported by a network of people focused on learning and improving. The willingness to lean in, solve problems, and support one another, as well as the team's work and growth, is critical to setting the team up for success.

This community-building requires intentional effort and systematic reinforcement. Consider implementing practices that strengthen collective capability and shared commitment:

- Create opportunities for informal connection and relationship-building
- Design collaborative problem-solving sessions that cross functional boundaries

- Establish mentoring circles that build networks of support
- Develop team rituals that celebrate collective achievements
- Structure work to require and reward collaboration
- Build in time for shared learning and reflection

As many researchers have established and practitioners have confirmed, teams built on the principles of community deliver faster and better results and share them more freely with others, creating a flywheel of ever-improving performance all around them.[219] [220] They can also do more with less, as strong communities naturally optimize resources and support one another through challenges. The mutual trust and understanding developed in a true community enables teams to adapt quickly, innovate more freely, and recover from setbacks more effectively.

For some great and engaging examples of this, see General McChrystal's book *Team of Teams*,[221] where he illustrates how building strong community connections enabled military units to become more agile and effective than traditional command-and-control structures could achieve.

Craft the Plan

Great things in business are never done by one person; they're done by a team of people. —Steve Jobs

While the work and research you put into understanding your organization and your mandate from Chapter 3 will set you up well to craft a plan, it will be your plan if you do it in isolation. What you truly need is a plan that belongs not only to you but also to your team. You need them as committed and "behind it" as you are. You should co-create an extraordinary future with meaningful work with your team, orchestrating the delivery of your true strategic potential. This jointly owned plan should include a combination of quick wins, significant investments, stages of work, and approaches to building political support in the organization.

We worked closely with a global technology executive, helping her craft a plan to transform the company's product and technology organization. It was an enormous undertaking with both strategic and operational challenges. She needed to create a deep partnership with the CEO and her C-level peers and ensure that she led everyone toward the same outcomes.

The plan we crafted divided tasks into categories similar to those we shared in Chapter 3, giving the team a clear understanding of how they organized their work to deliver on their mission.

- **Run the business:** lay down consistently improving operational results
  - o Establish clear performance baselines
  - o Set goals for improvement
  - o Deliver meaningful improvements
  - o Communicate the wins
  - o Master the processes (Strategy, operations & talent management)
- **Quick wins:** deliver short-term projects that capture real and immediate value
  - o Identify target quick wins
  - o Plan catalyzing initiatives and deliver them
  - o Communicate the wins and their bottom-line impact

- **BHAGs:** execute high value, mid-to-longer term projects
  - Articulate goals for future performance (BHAGs)
  - Gain wide-reaching alignment
  - Launch and execute projects to deliver against the BHAGs
  - Communicate the progress and results

In addition to these more traditional results-driven focus areas, we added a fourth focus centered on improving the organization's capabilities to improve continuously. Continuous improvement supports long-term success, and as understood and researched by Chris Argyris and Amy Edmondson,[222] [223] is tied to learning and growth. Organizations that have processes that foster learning and improvement dramatically outperform their peers and competitors. As a result, we added organizational transformation, focused on building learning and growth capabilities, to this list.

- **Organizational Transformation:** enhance skills, capabilities, and drive culture shifts
  - Set clear objectives for optimal organizational culture and capabilities
  - Plan for how to fully leverage, coach, redeploy, or release critical talent
  - Master the political system and how things really get done
  - Build allies and advocates

Once you have your thoughts on the above four focus areas, it's time to engage your team and any critical stakeholders to get everyone's input and co-create a plan of action to deliver on them.

One of the best ways to do this, which we have consistently found successful, is through large-scale working meetings to which the whole team is invited. We have leveraged several techniques, including those associated with Positive Organizational Scholarship (Quinn) and Appreciative Inquiry (Cooperrider), to help teams understand the root causes of their past success and potential improvement areas and craft a transformative future vision. The added benefit is engaging the group's power by co-creating your plan and ensuring deep understanding and buy-in to the path forward.

Once established, that vision can be built upon by fleshing out key actions in each focus area to manifest that future. Unlike other approaches, such large-scale meetings (sometimes called summits) can deliver both alignment and a detailed plan of action in 1-2 days rather than the weeks, months, or even years often required with more traditional disparate change management methods. High-level details of this framework can be found in Appendix 9A.

Your team is your force multiplier, and how you set them up will determine your and their success. With good leadership and some of these best practices, you should be able to deliver effectively on your joint mission.

Create Team Alignment

"Talent wins games, but teamwork and intelligence wins championships" —Michael Jordan

Most of today's work is done at the team level, and you will live or die by how effective your teams are.[224] As your team leader, you will need them to consistently deliver what matters most to the organization as a unit. Ensure they are clear on their objectives, well-aligned on priorities, and not fighting each other or the system. If your team fights one another, you, or the organization, winning becomes much more elusive. This challenge is amplified in today's hybrid work environment, where teams often collaborate across physical and virtual spaces.

Lead Authentically Across All Environments

Purpose-driven leaders find ways to maintain authentic connections regardless of physical distance. This approach fosters strong team dynamics by intentionally creating moments for genuine connection, even in virtual settings. Clear communication protocols ensure effective collaboration across all environments, while consistent transparency about challenges and opportunities builds trust. Making space for formal and informal interactions strengthens relationships, allowing for meaningful engagement beyond structured meetings. Thoughtfully leveraging technology enhances, rather than replaces, human connection, ensuring that teams remain cohesive and engaged regardless of their work environment.

The key is to maintain the human element in all interactions - in-person or virtual. This might mean starting virtual meetings with brief personal check-ins, establishing regular one-on-one virtual coffee chats, or creating digital spaces for spontaneous team interaction.

Maintain Alignment and Momentum

Best practice at the individual level is to focus on both the "what" (objectives) and the "how" (behaviors) when it comes to architecting a plan that optimizes outcomes.[225] [226] This framework, commonly used to align individual goals with organizational objectives, applies equally well to team leadership and performance management. It establishes a solid foundation for clear communication about priorities, timing, and what good looks like based on hard (KPIs) and soft (interpersonal) expectations. It also allows for highlighting gaps and identifying areas for continuous improvement.

The ultimate result is that everyone on the team has a clear and consistent understanding of what good looks like, what matters most to the organization, and how they are expected to operate if they are to be successful. This enables the whole team to come together in a context that allows them to work as one against a common enemy—the business and operating challenges they face.

Bringing Leadership Principles to Life

While understanding leadership principles is essential, the real impact comes from how you translate them into daily practices. Successful purpose-driven leaders select and adapt specific approaches that work for their context and culture. Here are examples of practices other leaders have used effectively, organized by key leadership principles. Consider these as a menu of options you can choose from, and then adapt approaches that will work best in your environment.

1. Setting Clear Direction

Clear direction requires consistent communication and reinforcement. Here are various approaches leaders have used successfully to maintain alignment from strategy to execution:

Daily Practices: Some effective daily touchpoints might include:
- Quick team huddles (many find 15 minutes sufficient)

- Brief end-of-day check-ins
- Just-in-time obstacle removal discussions

Weekly Rhythm: Weekly practices that often help maintain focus include:

- Team priority alignment sessions
- Cross-functional coordination touchpoints
- Key metric reviews

Monthly Cadence: Monthly reviews that many find valuable:

- Strategy implementation checkpoints
- Performance trend discussions
- Resource allocation adjustments

2. Building Engagement

Engagement flourishes when people feel connected to purpose, have a voice in the process, can help co-create solutions, and are valued for their contributions. Consider these approaches at different levels:

Individual Level - Successful approaches to personal connection include:

- Regular growth-focused conversations
- Discussions about meaningful work alignment
- Timely recognition of contributions

Team Level - Options for building team cohesion:

- Forums for sharing ideas and concerns
- Learning-focused team discussions
- Team achievement celebrations

Organizational Level - Ways to strengthen broader connection:

- Cross-functional collaboration opportunities

- Strategic impact discussions
- Purpose alignment conversations

3. Driving Performance Excellence

Excellence requires clear standards and support. Consider these components:

Setting Standards - Common approaches include:
- Defining clear expectations
- Establishing measurable outcomes
- Creating quality guidelines

Enabling Success - Support mechanisms might include:
- Resource planning
- Skill development opportunities
- Process improvement initiatives

Monitoring Progress - Effective feedback approaches include:
- Regular check-ins
- Data-informed discussions
- Adjustment opportunities

4. Supporting Growth and Development

Sustainable high-performance benefits from ongoing development. Consider these approaches:

Individual Growth - Development options might include:
- Personal development planning
- Stretch opportunities
- Mentoring connections

Team Capability - Team strengthening approaches:

- Skill-sharing opportunities
- Collective learning experiences
- Knowledge exchange forums

Organizational Learning - Systems that often support improvement:

- Practice sharing
- Innovation discussions
- Continuous improvement processes

Remember, the goal isn't to implement every practice but to thoughtfully select and adapt approaches that will work best in your context. Start with one or two practices that address your most pressing needs and build from there based on what works for your team and organization.

These leadership practices don't exist in isolation - they form part of the larger system we've explored throughout this book. They build upon the purpose-driven culture discussed in Chapter 6 and the optimized working methods we examined in Chapter 7. Combined with the executive perspective we covered in Chapter 8, these practices create a comprehensive approach to team leadership. By thoughtfully selecting and implementing practices that align with your purpose and values, you'll make a leadership approach that delivers immediate results and builds the foundation for sustainable success. As we'll explore in upcoming chapters, this integrated approach enables individual and organizational transformation.

Practical Implementation Example:

Sarah's story illustrates how these principles come together in practice. When she stepped in as CTO of a rapidly growing technology company, she inherited a challenging situation. Her organization struggled with siloed teams, unclear priorities, and inconsistent performance. Development cycles were unpredictable, team morale was suffering, and key customers were becoming frustrated with delivery delays.

"I knew we needed systematic change," Sarah reflected, "but I also knew we couldn't transform everything overnight." Instead of trying to implement every best practice at once, she started by understanding her team's pain points and identifying where small changes could make a meaningful impact.

Sarah began by establishing a clear weekly rhythm. She chose Monday mornings for strategy alignment, ensuring everyone understood their priorities and how they connected to larger organizational goals. Wednesdays became dedicated to cross-team coordination, allowing teams to share progress and surface dependencies. Friday afternoons were reserved for learning and planning, where teams could reflect on the week's achievements and challenges.

To support this rhythm, she implemented targeted feedback mechanisms. Daily metrics reviews helped teams stay focused on their most important outcomes. Weekly team pulse checks surfaced emerging issues before they became problems. Monthly deep dives allowed for thorough examination of trends and strategic adjustments.

Recognizing that sustainable improvement required investing in people, Sarah also built development infrastructure. She worked with HR to create skill-building programs aligned with individual aspirations and organizational needs. She established mentoring partnerships that crossed traditional department boundaries. Perhaps most importantly, she made career pathways visible and accessible to everyone.

The results surprised even Sarah. "We didn't just see improved metrics," she noted, "we saw a fundamental shift in how people worked together." Team alignment improved as people understood how their work connected to broader objectives. Engagement increased as individuals saw clear paths for growth and development. Performance outcomes organically improved as teams collaborated more effectively. Most notably, development cycles became more predictable, and customer satisfaction scores began trending upward.

"The key," Sarah emphasized, "was starting small and building momentum. We didn't try to boil the ocean. We selected a few key practices, implemented them well, and built from there." Her experience demonstrates how thoughtfully selected and consistently applied leadership practices can transform an organization.

Implementation Guidelines:

1. Start Small
   - Choose 1-2 practices to implement first
   - Build momentum through early wins
   - Add complexity gradually
2. Maintain Consistency
   - Stick to established rhythms
   - Honor commitments
   - Model desired behaviors
3. Gather Feedback
   - Ask for input regularly
   - Observe impact
   - Adjust as needed
4. Scale Successfully
   - Document what works

- Share learnings
- Expand thoughtfully

Remember, the goal isn't to implement every practice at once but to systematically build a leadership approach that brings your principles to life in meaningful ways. Start with the practices that will impact your context most and build from there.

Leading your team well creates an immediate impact. Now, let's ensure that the impact is sustainable by architecting your role for long-term success.

Key Chapter Takeaways

- Establish clear team priorities aligned with your mission.
- Energize and enable your team.
- Define both "what" your team should do and "how" they should operate.
- Co-create the plan of action with your team so that they not only understand it but also own it.

Chapter 9: Reflection Questions

1. How clear is your team about priorities and expectations?
2. What feedback mechanisms exist to support team performance?
3. How well aligned is your team with other functions?
4. Where could you provide more effective leadership support?

Chapter 10

Architect your role holistically

Clarify your focus	Invest in your capabilities	Deliver results
Connect with your purpose	Deepen purpose connection	Be an executive first
Asses the landscape	Upgrade your team	Lead with intention
Craft your vision	Tend to your culture	**Architect your role**
	Optimize ways of working	Practice agility

Style is a very simple matter; it is all rhythm. Once you get that, you can't use the wrong words. —Virginia Woolf

When your operating compass is centered and aligned with your true north, and you have a good balance (or at least rhythm) between all of the roles you must play, you get mojo – that "sweet spot" of performance and growth that gives you the right to a little swagger. It's balancing the personal, professional, and different focus areas at work. It involves navigating effectively the multiple organizational levels at which you need to operate.[227]

But it is not easy. In fact, it is among the most difficult challenges new executives face. They must simultaneously maintain healthy personal and professional boundaries while still delivering on their individual/

functional commitments and upholding their responsibilities as executives in the organization.

Consider Ann, a Strategy and Planning executive at a Fortune 500 financial services company. As an individual, she has personal and professional responsibilities and goals. As a functional team leader, she must provide direction, coaching, growth, and development, establishing an environment where her team can transform to meet new regulatory and competitive standards. Lastly, Ann has responsibilities as an executive of the company, taking on agendas and initiatives that benefit the company as a whole but span many functions, not just her own.

Neglecting any of these roles affects not only performance in that role but also has a long-term adverse effect on her ability to perform optimally in the other two roles. For example, she needs a solid working relationship and reputation for putting the company's interests first to garner the resources and support her departments and teams need. Similarly, she cannot deliver her agenda without a high-performing team supporting her. Operating at all three levels is not just a good thing but an absolute necessity.

As we discussed earlier, many executives prioritize their functional team leadership role, ensuring that those goals are delivered and, in doing so, neglect their individual and broader organizational responsibilities. They erroneously assume that delivering on their functional responsibilities will be sufficient. They do so at their peril as it not only impacts their ability in the short-term but also contributes to their long-term effectiveness and results in careers that derail, stagnate, or plateau.[228] [229] Executive leadership requires new thinking and skills, and the ability to create unity and cohesion, build teams, nurture interpersonal relationships, and adapt to transitions.

Consider Your Priorities

"To be mature you have to realize what you value most. It is extraordinary to discover that comparatively few people reach this level of maturity. They seem never to have paused to consider what has value for them. They spend great effort and sometimes make great sacrifices for values that, fundamentally, meet no real needs of their own. Perhaps they have imbibed the values of their particular profession or job, of their community or their neighbors, of their parents or family. Not to arrive at a clear understanding of one's own values is a tragic waste. You have missed the whole point of what life is for. "[230] —Eleanor Roosevelt

We have already discussed the importance of being true to yourself. This also extends to being honest with yourself about who you are, what motivates you, what matters to you, and what kind of life and legacy you want to create, personally and professionally. When we run on autopilot, we become a victim of our circumstances. As you consider your purpose, values, and what you want to be known for delivering, it is also crucial to be honest with yourself and consider not just what you want to do but how.

Stay grounded in your vision/purpose, values, and strengths. Then, be honest about what's working and what's not. Most challenges boil down to at least one of these things being out of alignment. This is ultimately about maintaining alignment among these three things and creating an appropriate set of rhythms and routines that support this alignment across your many different roles.

We often hear longings about work-life balance, lamenting that it is a desirable but elusive goal. Morbidly, work/life balance implies an either-or competition between the two. You are either working or you are living. If you think about it, that's a pretty depressing way to consider our time at work. Like many other working parents, we think work-life balance is a myth - it doesn't exist. What we believe is essential, and does exist, is the ability to intelligently consider how you allocate your time to ensure that it is consistent with your values and maximizes your return on invested time. For Dreama Walton, an ultramarathon runner, Melissa works with, that includes setting aside hours of her week to train while protecting time with her daughter and pursuing a satisfying career. For others, that might mean putting in 80-hour work weeks to ensure they reach the next rung on the corporate ladder. The point is that there is no single correct answer, but each of us must choose where to allocate our time in a way consistent with what is most essential to us while balancing our needs and those of the stakeholders in our lives.

Adopt a Work-Life Integration Mindset

A healthier perspective is to consider the construct of work/life integration. This framework allows us to take a more holistic perspective on the work, home, family, community, personal well-being, spiritual, and health aspects of our lives. When we are working (consider the ways we can fulfill larger purposes than ourselves, solve problems, serve others, build relationships, and enjoy moments), we are living. Aren't we?

We must care for our personal, spiritual, emotional, physical, and relational well-being. How we integrate these aspects throughout our days will look different for each of us. And it will invariably be different on any given day. We certainly need to set healthy boundaries regarding our work activities. That's perhaps even more true now, with many of us working at least part-time from home. Setting healthy boundaries is valid for everything, not just work. We challenge the notion that any boundaries we put around work ought to insinuate that we are no longer in our lives for half of our day. That's absurd, right?

Our traditional thinking about work/life balance similarly affects our own resilience. It seduces us into subconsciously putting a big black-box around half of our life that robs us of the ability to achieve a greater sense of synergy and meaningfulness.

At first blush, you might dismiss the swapping of "work/life balance" for "work/life integration" as trivial semantics. But the words we use matter. They infuse themselves into our subconscious, permeate our psyche, and ultimately influence how we experience our socially constructed world.

The phrase "work/life balance" is well-intentioned but also misinformed. It's analogous to praising a child for being smart versus praising them for effort. Research has demonstrated that this common practice, while well-intentioned, is detrimental to children's development of resilience.[231]

Our traditional thinking about work/life balance similarly affects our resilience. It seduces us into subconsciously putting a big black box around half of our lives, robbing us of achieving greater synergy and meaningfulness.

It's essential to mindfully integrate the various aspects of our lives because everything we do is living. We don't, or shouldn't, pause living when we go to work. Optimally, we will enjoy our work and find it meaningful. But even if we are in a job that provides little satisfaction other than a paycheck, we do ourselves a disservice when holding onto a work/life balance mindset because it limits our potential.

Reflect on your own life and vocation. Discard the "work/life balance" framework and instead embrace "work/life integration". Be mindful of your activities, inside and outside of work, and assess what seems to be working well for you, how work integrates with your whole life, and what might warrant adjustment. And live your whole days.

Liberation Through Integration

The pressure to have all the answers can be exhausting and ultimately counterproductive. As discussed earlier, purpose-driven leaders understand that their role isn't to be the smartest person in the room but to create conditions where collective wisdom can flourish. They crowdsource success. This mindset isn't just liberating for your team but for you as a leader.

When you stop trying to be superhuman at work, you create space for being more fully human in all aspects of life. This might mean:

- Being present with family rather than mentally solving work problems
- Pursuing interests that energize and renew you
- Building relationships outside your professional circle
- Taking care of your physical and mental well-being
- Engaging in your broader community

Consider Sarah, a technology executive we worked with, who discovered that delegating more responsibility to her team improved their performance and allowed her to be more present with her teenage children during a crucial period in their lives. Her willingness to let go of control paradoxically gave her more influence at work and home. This aligns with research showing that leaders who effectively integrate their work and personal lives create more sustainable success patterns.[232]

Engage Your Best Self

We have advised, mentored, and coached hundreds of executives, and we see one thing repeatedly. Without realizing it, many of these leaders focus so much on trying to be what they think their boards, investors, customers, strategic partners, or even their significant others want them to be that they lose their sense of self. It is not surprising really - we are wired for belonging. As a result, we can expend too much energy trying to be a version of ourselves that meets the expectations of others, but may run counter to what we are at our core. Consequently, we struggle with priorities, doubt, and focus, never genuinely finding our footing.

Alex, the founder of an Australian company, Mindful Collective, fell into the trap of losing herself early in her launch by trying to be something she wasn't. She had been inspired to launch her company after her own experience with postpartum depression, and when she spoke about it, her energy and passion were palpable. That energy and her vibrant voice came through in her marketing materials. Yet, they were completely absent from an initial, sterilized pitch deck she had prepared for prospective seed funding.

She acknowledged that she had let her initial lack of confidence get the better of her, losing her unique and powerful voice as she tried to contort herself and articulate her company value in the way she thought investors wanted. In attempting to be what she thought she was supposed to be, she lost what made her company and pitch so impactful. When she moved through her fear and leaned into her voice, the pitch reflected the business's strengths, allowing her and her company to shine.

Alex was "catering" to her audience, reshaping herself to her audience's perceived expectations. While on the surface, it seems like a clever tactic that will maximize positive results, doing so often minimizes our impact and carries a cognitive and emotional load that can undermine our performance. The irony here is that since we can't be sure about the preferences and expectations of our audience, it heightens our anxiety and makes us come across as phony. Coming across as inauthentic decreases our effectiveness, with studies suggesting a significant drop in positive outcomes when people cater to their audiences.

If, as Stephen M.R. Covey asserts, business moves at the speed of trust,[233] we must consider how it is built. Investors, boards, customers, peers, and employees look for leaders who are the "real deal" and whose values resonate with their own. So, do your best to be you to avoid coming across as phony and undermining the trust you are attempting to build. Once you are grounded in your strengths and priorities, it is easier to articulate and act upon them.

Map Out Your Time

The next challenge is investing and allocating your time wisely. We helped a Chief Product and Technology officer onboard at a new company a few years back. One of the most important things we did was examine her responsibilities, transformation agenda, and goals and objectives. With that in mind, we mapped out the optimal way she should invest her limited time and what each set of tasks would require.

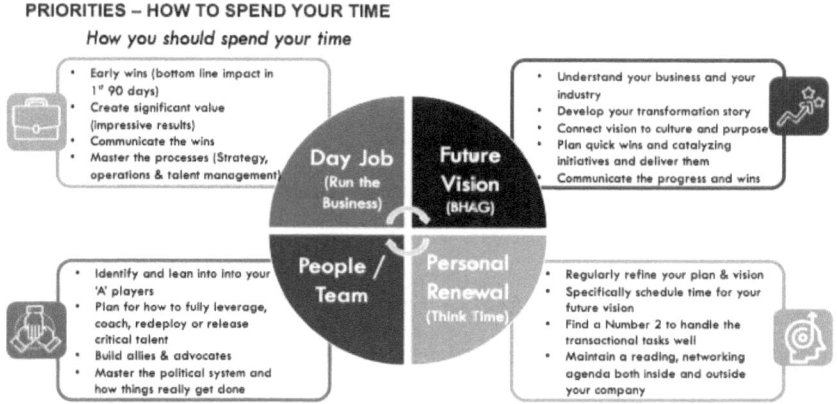

We divided her role into four categories of responsibility that parallel the team focus areas, each with objectives. We suggested she color-code her calendar and plan her week to balance these tasks.

It generally worked like the food pyramid plan we were introduced to as kids. No single day would look perfect, but when she scanned her monthly calendar, she saw she had a good distribution of time spent on each activity category. The visual helped her think of how to allocate her time, and color-coding her calendar kept her honest. It enabled her to ensure she was not neglecting important things in favor of things that felt urgent. Specifically, it kept her from falling into the trap of foregoing time to think strategically, kept her network strong, and nurtured the capabilities that allowed her to be the strategic innovation leader her company desperately needed.

Below are the four categories we recommended for her and have generally found helpful for most executives. We have also included suggested items you may consider during those first 90 days to establish your rhythms and routines.

1. Day Job (Running the business)
- Early wins (bottom line impact in 1st 90 days)
- Create significant value (impressive results)
- Communicate the wins
- Master the processes (Strategy, operations & talent management)

2. Future Vision (BHAG)
- Understand your business and your industry
- Develop your transformation story
- Connect vision to culture and purpose
- Plan quick wins and catalyzing initiatives, then deliver them
- Communicate the progress and wins

3. People / Team (Networks, Leadership & Team building)
- Identify and lean into your 'A' players
- Plan for how to fully leverage, coach, redeploy, or release critical talent
- Build allies & advocates
- Master the political system and how things really get done

4. Personal Renewal (Think time)
- Regularly refine your plan & vision
- Specifically, schedule time for your future vision
- Find a Number 2 to handle the transactional tasks well
- Maintain a reading and networking agenda both inside and outside your company

While the first three categories focus on delivering organizational value, the fourth category - Personal Renewal - is often overlooked yet crucial for sustainable leadership. Many executives treat renewal as optional, something to be addressed after everything else is handled. However, research shows this approach ultimately undermines personal and organizational effectiveness.

Personal Renewal: Sustaining Your Leadership Energy

While strategic thinking time is crucial, sustainable leadership requires holistic renewal. Research shows that executives who maintain their effectiveness long-term actively manage their energy across multiple dimensions:[234]

Physical Renewal

- Prioritize sleep and recovery
- Maintain regular exercise
- Schedule breaks between intense periods
- Practice healthy eating habits
- Honor vacation time

Mental Renewal

- Carve out dedicated thinking time
- Engage in strategic reflection
- Read widely outside your industry
- Learn new skills or perspectives
- Find a Number 2 to handle transactional tasks

Emotional Renewal

- Build strong personal relationships
- Maintain interests outside work
- Practice mindfulness or meditation
- Set healthy boundaries
- Engage in activities that bring joy

Spiritual/Purpose Renewal

- Stay connected to your 'why'
- Contribute to your community
- Mentor others
- Reflect on impact and legacy
- Align actions with values

Many executives neglect these renewal practices, seeing them as luxuries they can't afford. However, research demonstrates that leaders who make renewal a priority show greater resilience, make better decisions, and maintain their effectiveness longer.[235] As one CEO we worked with observed, 'I finally realized that taking care of myself wasn't selfish - it was essential to taking care of my team and organization.'

Practical Implementation: Integrating Renewal Into Your Leadership Practice

Translating renewal principles into daily practice requires intentional planning and consistent execution.

Start by blocking dedicated renewal time in your calendar, treating these appointments with the same importance as key business meetings. Create structured morning and evening routines that support your well-being, providing bookends to your day that ensure you maintain energy and perspective.

Gradually build renewal habits into your weekly schedule, identifying specific activities that replenish your physical, mental, emotional, and purpose-driven energy.

To maintain commitment, find accountability partners for key renewal practices who can provide support and honest feedback.

Finally, regularly assess and adjust your renewal approach based on changing circumstances and personal insights, recognizing that effective renewal practices evolve as your leadership journey progresses.

Remember: Your capacity to lead effectively is directly tied to your ability to make it sustainable. Make renewal non-negotiable in your schedule.

Integrate Your Leadership Practices

With these renewal practices, you're better positioned to execute across all four categories. Just as airlines remind us to 'put on your own oxygen mask before helping others,' maintaining personal sustainability enables you to better serve your team and organization. This foundation of renewal supports your ability to think strategically, lead effectively, and maintain the energy needed for long-term success.

If you are stepping into a new role or organization, integrate these elements into your 100-day plan (see Chapter 3 for detailed planning frameworks and templates). Suppose you have followed our advice from prior chapters. In that case, you have already designed your work and that of your team so that you have feedback loops and coordination across the organization, with cascading actions, strategies, and plans.

While these renewal practices are essential, implementing them alongside demanding business responsibilities can feel overwhelming. Many executives struggle to protect time for strategic thinking and renewal while managing daily operations. One executive we coached faced this exact challenge - he needed to compartmentalize and balance near- and long-term considerations while maintaining stakeholder alignment and effective communication. The following framework helped him shape his thinking and identify specific actions:

For each of these categories, we captured actions to maintain/nurture, start or consider, and those to avoid (full framework in Appendix 10B):

1. Keep the Runway Clear: Contain & Delegate Urgent/Pressing Issues
2. Build the Rules for the Airways: Establish Timing, Cadence, Structure, and Processes
3. Communicate with the Control Tower: Ensure and Manage the Board
4. Establish the Flight Plan(s): Set the Vision & Strategy
5. Maintain On-time Flight Performance: Run the Business/ Programs

Put It Into Practice

At this point, you have thought through your time, priorities, key work that needs to be delivered, and the critical work, meetings, and discussions you need to have happen. We have also discussed hardwiring in the relationships you need to nurture to succeed. Now, you're ready to tackle the rhythms you operate by and hardwire into your schedule a plan for balancing the work you need to do at the individual, team, and organizational levels.

As always, the best practice is to stay grounded in your purpose, values, mission, and personal goals. These provide the ideal guardrails for your goals. If you lay them out annually, you can reverse engineer quarterly targets that can be assessed (and potentially recalibrated) as the year progresses. In your quarterly plan, think carefully about what you want to accomplish in that window and what you hope to transform, improve, or deliver.

Find Your Flow

Now that you've got everything laid out, take a step back and consider its mechanics and practicality. This is ultimately about finding rhythms that work for you and allow you to get into that zone of consistent high performance that many refer to as a state of personal flow.[236] [237] It can be tempting to rigorously apply these frameworks and principles, overschedule yourself, and miss the opportunity to create flow. So, this is where you need to experiment with what works for you, make real-time adjustments, and figure out what works best for you.

For some, that means setting aside blocks of time and grouping similar tasks. For others, it's spreading out team meetings and one-on-ones evenly across the week. Maybe it's hardwiring in an afternoon "tea" break or mid-morning walking meetings. Whatever works for you, lean into it, and be ready to adapt as you learn and evolve.

Architecting for Sustainability

The ultimate measure of your leadership isn't just what you achieve during your tenure but what continues after you move on.[238] Achieving sustainable success requires balancing multiple timeframes, ensuring immediate results and future growth. Daily execution excellence keeps operations running smoothly and efficiently, while medium-term capability building strengthens skills, processes, and team development. At the same time, focusing on long-term legacy creation ensures that decisions contribute to a lasting impact, reinforcing organizational values and strategic vision over time.

Research shows that leaders who successfully balance these horizons create more resilient organizations.[239] The key is maintaining a clear connection to purpose while building systems that support sustainable performance. As Cameron and Quinn[240] note, organizations that maintain excellence over time have leaders who consciously architect for sustainability.

This approach ensures long-term success by creating scalable and adaptable processes, allowing organizations to evolve with changing needs. Building leadership capability at all levels fosters a culture of empowerment and resilience while establishing feedback loops that drive continuous improvement and innovation. Maintaining key cultural elements strengthens organizational identity and cohesion, ensuring that core values endure over time. Above all, keeping purpose at the center of decision-making aligns actions with a shared vision, reinforcing commitment and sustained growth.

Maintaining this broader perspective while staying grounded in purpose can create impact that ripples far beyond your immediate sphere of influence. Your role as an executive provides unique opportunities to shape not just today's results, but tomorrow's possibilities.

With your role well-defined, the final piece is ensuring you and your organization can adapt and thrive in an ever-changing environment. This requires building agility into your leadership approach.

Key Chapter Takeaways

- Craft the blueprint for your executive role.
- Establish a leadership style that aligns with your vision.
- Define your responsibilities and set priorities to facilitate both effectiveness and balance.

Chapter 10 Reflection Questions

1. What systems do you have for capturing and sharing learnings?
2. How agile is your approach to change and adaptation?
3. Where might you need external support or perspective?
4. What habits will help sustain your leadership effectiveness?

Chapter 11

Practice agility for long-term success

Clarify your focus	Invest in your capabilities	Deliver results
Connect with your purpose	Deepen purpose connection	Be an executive first
Asses the landscape	Upgrade your team	Lead with intention
Craft your vision	Tend to your culture	Architect your role
	Optimize ways of working	**Practice agility**

"Success is not final, failure is not fatal: It is the courage to continue that counts." —Winston Churchill

The journey doesn't end with success; it evolves. Explore strategies for sustained success, continuous improvement, and personal and professional growth. Develop a roadmap that ensures your leadership legacy endures long after your initial triumphs.

Remember - Yesterday's Performance Won't Meet Today's Goals

Once you have your plan and are focused on delivering it, it can be tempting to put your head down and execute the heck out of it. Unfortunately, we live in a VUCA (volatile, uncertain, complex, and ambiguous) world; the only true constant is change. So, things will continue to shift and evolve as internal, geopolitical, and market realities change, requiring consistent awareness and adaptation.

The most significant and surprisingly consistent insight from investors like Warren Buffett, authors like James Clear (Atomic Habits), and Harvard researchers studying happiness,[241] [242] is the single common[243] truth that small, nearly imperceptible improvements, when consistently applied, yield the best results. Buffett famously suggested the secret to investment success was a small snowball (money) and a long hill (gradual but consistent gains).[244] When aspiring to achieve extraordinary performance, a key question is how you consistently identify and apply the right actions.

You can't simply adopt a "set it and forget it" mindset. Ultimately, it comes down to you and those around you operating with an agile, learning mindset.

Breaking Through Performance Plateaus

"If you really look closely,
most overnight successes took a long time." —Steve Jobs

The journey to high performance, whether in sports or business, requires systematic approaches to breaking through plateaus. Consider this journey of pushing past perceived limitations:

When Patrick first attempted endurance sports, he could barely complete six minutes of a spin class. Like many leaders facing new challenges, his initial response was to retreat from the discomfort. But watching a 76-

year-old cancer survivor complete a triathlon challenged his assumptions about what was possible and inspired him to push beyond his comfort zone.

His first attempt at open water swimming during a race ended in failure—a common experience for leaders taking on new challenges without adequate preparation. Rather than letting this setback define his limits, he used it as data to inform a more systematic approach to improvement. Just as leaders must build capabilities methodically, he broke down the challenge into manageable components: first mastering pool swimming, then adding open water practice, and finally integrating race conditions.

When facing his next significant challenge - a half Ironman - he encountered what many leaders face: the reality that previous approaches, while successful for smaller challenges, weren't sufficient for this new level of performance. The choppy waters of Lake Erie overwhelmed his existing capabilities, much like how leaders often find that strategies that worked for smaller organizations or more straightforward challenges don't scale to more complex situations.

Instead of abandoning the goal, he adjusted his approach. He engaged a coach for external perspective and expertise - a practice many successful leaders employ. He joined a training group that practiced in challenging conditions, similar to how organizations build capabilities through deliberate practice in controlled but realistic situations. Most importantly, he established a systematic approach to improvement with explicit feedback loops and measurement.

The parallel to organizational leadership is clear: breakthrough performance requires systematic approaches to pushing beyond current capabilities. Just as athletes can't simply try harder using the same techniques, organizations can't achieve new performance levels by working longer hours with existing processes. Both require a structured approach with clear goal setting to provide direction and focus.

Systematic capability building ensures continuous skill development, while regular feedback loops drive ongoing improvement. Gaining an external perspective helps challenge assumptions and inspire new ideas, while deliberate practice hones expertise over time. Finally, persistence through setbacks is essential, allowing individuals and teams to overcome obstacles and sustain progress toward their objectives.

This brings us to a practical framework for breaking through performance plateaus in your organization that we outline here:

1. Set Clear Goals:

Define specific, measurable, achievable, relevant, and time-bound (SMART) goals. Knowing precisely what you want to achieve is the first step to breaking through a plateau.

Each time Patrick signs up to complete a race, he creates a detailed commitment with clear goals: the type of race, the associated distances, and the time available to prepare.

2. Reflect and Identify the Plateau:

Take time to assess your current performance and understand where you're plateauing. Are there specific skills or areas where you're stuck? Pinpoint the issues you need to address.

When Patrick failed to complete his first half-Ironman, it was evident that he needed to work on open-water swimming and the mental training associated with it.

3. Seek Feedback and Inspiration:

Reach out to mentors, peers, or experts in your field for feedback on your performance. They can provide valuable insights and suggestions for improvement.

Patrick sought feedback and inspiration from friends and peers who had completed the half Ironman and worked formally with his coach to prepare a training plan and debrief his progress.

4. Analyze and Adjust Your Strategy:

Review your current strategies and identify what's not working. Be willing to adjust your approach and try new methods to overcome the plateau.

In conversation with his coach and analysis of his training data, Patrick was able to make appropriate tweaks to his training plan along the way.

5. Break Your Goal into Smaller Steps:

Often, plateaus occur because our goals are too overwhelming. Break them down into smaller, more manageable steps. You may find ways to gamify this work. This can make your progress more tangible and achievable.

Patrick didn't set out to go from couch to half Ironman in one season (though some people certainly do). He set his training plan for the month with his coach and made appropriate adjustments as needed. However, his focus was always on one workout at a time. Even in a given workout, he breaks larger workouts into smaller sub-goals on which to focus (e.g., this set of 10 laps at the pool, then the next, etc.).

6. Consistent Practice and Effort:

Plateaus often result from a lack of consistent effort. Dedicate time each day or week to working on specific skills or tasks to reach your goals.

Half the battle is showing up. Patrick trained every day (with active recovery days as part of his regimen), and once in the habit, it merely became an automatic part of his routine.

7. Cross-Training and Diversification:

Explore related skills or fields that can complement your primary area of focus. Cross-training and diversification can provide fresh perspectives and help you break through plateaus.

The sport of triathlon has inherent cross-training, which minimizes the risk of injury and enhances overall health. These benefits carry over to other aspects of life and work, such as strengthening commitment, discipline, and mindfulness.

8. Visualization and Mental Training:

Use visualization techniques to rehearse success and imagine yourself mentally breaking through the plateau. Positive mental reinforcement is a critically important tool.

In Patrick's case, he visualized completing each leg of the race hundreds of times as he trained. By the time the race arrived, Patrick was merely living out what he had already achieved in his mind. Conversely, when he did not complete the race, he had not mentally trained sufficiently for the challenge.

9. Stay Accountable:

Share your goals and progress with a trusted friend, coach, or mentor who can help hold you accountable. Knowing someone is watching can provide extra motivation.

Whenever he felt the urge to let up in a workout or take a pass, Patrick knew that his coach would see his workout data (or lack thereof). He also advertised his goal to friends and family, providing additional motivation and accountability.

10. Be Patient and Persistent:

Breaking through a performance plateau can take time. Stay patient and persistent. Celebrate small victories along the way, and don't be discouraged by setbacks.

Patrick's first half Ironman attempt was unsuccessful, but it motivated him and helped him adapt and adjust his plan so he could complete it the next time.

Breaking through plateaus is a journey. It will not happen overnight. The key is staying committed to your goals, remaining adaptable, and pushing your boundaries to achieve new performance levels.

Maintain Agility at Scale

As organizations grow, they often lose the nimbleness that enabled their early success. The same is true for leaders and teams. Systems become more complex, decisions slow down, and bureaucracy creeps in. Purpose-driven leaders actively work to prevent this organizational hardening.

Consider how Amazon has maintained its 'Day 1' mentality despite massive growth. Jeff Bezos consistently emphasized quick decision-making, customer obsession, and willingness to experiment.[245] This approach allows large organizations to maintain startup-like agility by prioritizing speed and adaptability in decision-making.

Rather than waiting for complete certainty, leaders make informed choices with about 70% of ideal information, enabling faster action. Empowering front-line teams to operate without excessive approval layers fosters responsiveness and innovation. Small, autonomous teams enhance agility, allowing the organization to move quickly in response to changing conditions. Companies stay aligned with market demands by maintaining a strong focus on customer needs rather than internal bureaucracy. Continuous feedback loops facilitate rapid course correction, ensuring sustained progress and competitiveness.

The key is designing systems that support rather than impede agility - creating systems that enable, rather than hinder, swift decision-making and action. This involves simplifying approval processes to remove bottlenecks and eliminating unnecessary meetings and reports that slow productivity. Clearly defining decision rights at appropriate levels ensures that the right people can act without unnecessary delays. Maintaining a direct connection to customers and the market keeps the organization responsive to real-world needs. Additionally, regularly pruning outdated processes prevents bureaucracy from creeping in, allowing the company to remain nimble and focused on what truly drives success.

As one technology executive we worked with observed, 'Every quarter, we ask ourselves: What processes are helping us serve customers better, and what processes are just making us feel better about being in control?'

Adopt an Agile Learning Mindset

No plan survives first contact with the enemy.
—Field Marshall Helmuth von Moltke

To borrow an encouragement from Todd Herman, professional mindset coach to entrepreneurs and elite athletes, it's critical to "get on the field of play". You've spent some important time reflecting on how you will show up as a leader so that you can take more intentional action to move forward. But, it's essential to make sure that you balance being mindful and intentional with taking accurate and appropriate action, and avoid paralysis by analysis.

Instead of over-analyzing and overthinking to the point that you don't generate value and miss opportunities to learn, put the wheels in motion and prepare to learn through action. As discussed in Chapter 6, the psychological safety you've built provides the foundation for this kind of productive experimentation. When teams feel safe to take risks and learn from mistakes, they can move faster and innovate more effectively. This creates a virtuous cycle where each learning experience builds capability and confidence.

The best way to learn is to be in action, doing the work of innovating, experimenting, and engaging. This may take the form of developing a prototype to get feedback from a customer, developing an MVP to bring to market, or getting feedback from an internal partner on a new process. To the extent that your product, service, or key-value delivery systems can be developed or modified iteratively with an agile mindset, the less wasted time you will have and the more forward traction you will develop.

Once you've improved the prototype, product, or process, establishing a process that invites team members to appropriately engage in garnering feedback and optimizing the design and implementation will improve their ability to innovate and dramatically improve accountability. People support what they help to create, and the increased sense of ownership extends to the implementation and ongoing optimization.

On a recent trip to the beach, Melissa had the pleasure of observing a surfing lesson. The first class was taught on the solid sandy beach, where a whole class of wannabe surfers adroitly followed the instructor's instructions. As directed, they laid down on their surfboards and got their feet and hands into the correct positions to get themselves upright and into the classic surfer pose. They had done it, mastered getting onto the surfboard, and were ready to hit the waves.

But, they quickly discovered that what was easy on solid ground was not as easy as bouncing atop a sea of waves. All their carefully practiced skills and plans were helpful. Still, it became clear that constant adjustments and recalibrations would be required to successfully get up and expertly ride the waves in the volatile and changing environment they found in the real world of surfing.

The same can be said of our professional roles. Plans are undoubtedly critical to determining how we should proceed. Still, scholars at HBS and MIT have substantiated that the value of planning is not just the strategies and plans but also the skills that we develop in putting them together. Having gone through the exercise of putting together the plan has helped your team buy into the plan and get on board. But it has also helped them develop skills to be better leaders and adjust on the fly.[246]

According to Harvard researchers,[247][248] true agility is achieved when we effectively manage complex situations along several dimensions. We have already discussed the contributing factors to building your team and culture to drive success. Many of these factors will also ensure agility, such as staffing your team with collaborative experts, aligning on an inspiring shared ambition, establishing a culture of learning and engagement, and providing sufficient autonomy augmented by strong leader support.

Some of these factors, however, involve building flexibility into your plans, rhythms, and routines. Three key principles are necessary to maintain agility in your planning:

1. focusing on the right activities in the right mix while ensuring alignment across multiple stakeholders creates strategic coherence and efficiency;

2. adaptive roadmaps allow flexibility in response to changing conditions and emerging opportunities; and

3. designing dynamic feedback loops ensures that new information is continuously integrated, enabling ongoing refinement and improvement.

Together, these principles create a planning framework that is both structured and responsive, balancing strategic direction with the ability to pivot as needed.

In reality, the first of these principles is relatively easy and logical for most leaders; it's what we've learned to do over our careers. Suppose you have a highly complex operating process that is difficult to balance. In that case, you may find it helpful to engage a consultative partner or tap into the work of thought leaders on process and project management.

Most leaders must ensure agility in these key areas—their roadmaps and feedback loops. We recommend designing two types of review triggers to hard-wire in opportunities for learning and course correction: schedule- and event-driven triggers.

Schedule-driven triggers are reviews and data-gathering exercises planned at certain scheduled intervals, typically every two to four weeks for operating KPIs and one to three months for customer feedback-driven KPIs.

Event-driven triggers, by contrast, are initiated automatically when a KPI hits a certain level (e.g., when trading is halted if volume or price drops hit certain levels on Wall Street) or when a certain point in the project is reached (e.g., a phase is completed). Establishing both triggers ensures a regular opportunity to reassess, reevaluate, and course-correct as new information or opportunities arise.

Say Yes to the Mess

Unfortunately, even the best-laid plans can't control every bit of chaos; that is when we must embrace the messy reality and find a way to work with it. As Frank Barrett encourages in the title of his book, "Say Yes to the Mess."[249] He draws parallels between work and jazz.

In jazz improvisation, there are no carefully written sheets of music; each team member has a critical and complementary role in listening to others as they add to the group's music. It requires responding to and working with the uncertainty and change you are presented with. Musicians, like leaders, ultimately learn, grow, and improve as they gain experience if they remain open-minded. Just as staying true to a key or style of music roots musicians during improv sessions, staying true to your purpose and vision will help you move through the inevitable challenging periods of uncertainty or complexity.

Action is inherently messy. But if you encourage a learning culture of experimentation and create boundary conditions to allow this sandbox play, you can deliver incredible performance. This play will be the birthplace of new and innovative ideas that will surprise and delight your customers and become the lifeblood of your company.

Find Your Mojo

> *"You're not the average of the FIVE people you surround yourself with. It's way bigger than that. You're the average of all the people who surround you. So take a look around and make sure you're in the right surroundings."* —David Burkus

We are wired to be social creatures, and communities add significant value to business leaders. From providing tangible support resources to mentoring support and accountability to strategic relationships to help accelerate growth, there are numerous benefits to being in a community. There are also numerous choices—from trade associations or industry groups to chambers of commerce to countless online communities focused on similar pursuits.

One specific type of community we encourage you to consider is aligning yourself with a peer group with whom you can be more fully transparent. We have been members of various peer groups for nearly two decades and have seen the enormous value they provide. They provide helpful advice as you work through various business challenges, whether this is merely additional moral support and accountability (do not underestimate the power of this alone) or thought partnership.

As an additional encouragement, we are strong proponents of business coaching/advisory support and recommend enlisting the services of a business coach with whom you are well-aligned to help in all of these areas we've explored in this journey together. If you don't already have a coach, get one—but be sure to look for a good fit. The support, clarity, and accountability you can realize with a business coach who is a good fit for you will make the investment well worth it.

Share Key Learnings

Lastly, and possibly most importantly, the best leaders ensure that they take an agile learning approach within their teams and departments and spearhead a system for sharing learnings across the organization.

MIT's Steven Spear[250][251] highlights the value of curating systematic approaches to sharing knowledge and the actual value they create for the organizations that use them. He has studied the long-term competitive value created in various industries, including military, healthcare, manufacturing, and drug development. His findings confirm that continuous improvement, fueled by learning, helps organizations outperform their peers over the long term.

Systems that capture and share knowledge support sustainable competitive advantage. As a leader, one of the most important ways to do this is to encourage experimentation so that teams learn from their mistakes and share those learnings as widely as possible.

Key Chapter Takeaways

- Yesterday's performance won't meet today's goals.
- Adopt an agile, learning mindset.
- Design in dynamic feedback loops.
- Get a good executive coach in your corner.
- Share learnings across the organization.

Chapter 11 Reflection Questions - Bringing Everything Together

Personal Agility & Learning

1. How comfortable are you with ambiguity and constant change?
2. What are your current practices for continuous learning and improvement?
3. Where do you tend to get stuck in "analysis paralysis" versus taking action?

Systems & Processes

1. What feedback loops currently exist in your organization?
2. How effectively do you capture and share learnings across teams?
3. What barriers prevent quick adaptation to new information or circumstances?

Leadership Sustainability

1. What support systems do you have in place for your growth?
2. How do you balance maintaining stability while driving change?

3. Where might you need additional resources or perspectives?

Team Development

1. How well does your team embrace experimentation and learning?
2. What mechanisms exist for your team to share and implement improvements?
3. How do you currently celebrate and learn from both successes and failures?

Future Focus

1. What emerging trends or changes might impact your organization?
2. How prepared is your team to adapt to unexpected challenges?
3. What capabilities need development to ensure long-term success?

Implementation Planning

1. Which of your current practices need to become more agile?
2. What specific changes could help your team learn and adapt faster?
3. How will you measure progress in building organizational agility?

Support Network

1. Who are your key advisors and mentors?
2. What communities or networks could enhance your learning?
3. How might external perspectives help your development?

Conclusion

We began writing this book to try and answer the question many executives struggle with as they step into new challenges, "How do I succeed in this new role?" Having had a ringside seat to many incredible successes and a few failures, we wondered if developing a playbook could increase the likelihood of success.

In particular, we were looking for tools, techniques, and approaches that would equip every leader to thrive while building the conditions in which their teams and organizations would realize incredible results. Through our own experiences and work, interviews with a broad swath of leaders, and our study of academic research, we have curated what we believe are the best practices.

The central, but often overlooked, differentiator is the power of purpose and its potential to unify and propel great success. Embracing and leveraging an organization's purpose catalyzes action, transforming the mundane into meaningful work, and energizing the organization to achieve greatness. Extraordinary leaders connect their purpose to all their strategic and tactical organizational decisions.

In addition, these great leaders create environments that unlock the full potential of those around them. They develop plans and innovate with their teams rather than for them, leveraging the organization's collective wisdom and experience and building engagement and buy-in. These leaders also create organizations that learn and grow, ensuring that today's wins are only a starting point as they look toward setting new standards in the future.

The leadership journey isn't simple or easy, and there will be many hurdles along the way, including transforming legacy systems, building new capabilities, and delivering on aggressive timelines. But the real challenges, and ultimately the real victories, come from how you and your team approach them.

Sarah, a CTO whose leadership journey we both studied and supported, highlights the power of the approach we have described. She stepped into an organization full of legacy systems, competitive pressures, and a need to deliver results quickly. It was overwhelming, and the issues were almost insurmountable. But she leaned into the organization's purpose, charted a path toward transformation, and engaged her team in crafting solutions. That was the easy part.

The real challenge was sticking to that approach when her team struggled with a critical platform migration. In that high-stakes, high-stress moment, when senior leadership was challenging their method, she made a pivotal choice to double down on this approach.

Instead of pushing harder on timelines and metrics, she had gathered her team to reground on their purpose - enabling small businesses to thrive in an increasingly digital world. That moment shifted everything.

Engineers who had been focused on technical specifications began thinking about the shop owners who would use their solution. Project managers who had been tracking deadlines started considering business impact. The team didn't just deliver a platform; they created tools that transformed their customers' businesses.

That pivotal moment drove fundamental transformation and incredible results—improved performance, higher customer satisfaction, and increased market share. However, Sarah measured their actual achievement with a longer-term lens. She saw it in how her team collaborated, their pride in discussing customer success stories, and how they had grown as leaders. She understood that this one success was just the beginning, as they had built the capabilities to deliver consistent growth well into the future.

She described the lessons she took away from this moment with a quote from one of her earliest mentors: "Leadership isn't about being in charge; it's about taking care of those in your charge." The wisdom of those words had proven true time and again, not just for Sarah but for great leaders everywhere.

Purpose-driven leadership delivers results and creates an environment where people can do their best work in service of something meaningful. It creates an upward cycle of performance, meaning, and success that builds upon itself.

It allows leaders, teams, and organizations to face significant challenges confidently—not because they have all the answers, but because they are grounded in their purpose, committed to the journey together, and have built an engine for learning, growth, and success.

Bring It All Together and Move Forward

Leadership can be difficult, and stepping into a new executive role is undoubtedly one of the most challenging. We hope that the insights and techniques we have shared will help you step in and step up to that challenge, knowing that your purpose and values can fuel your success. These best practices (and cautionary tales) are a strong foundation to draw from, whether you are an experienced executive looking to tweak your approach or a new executive feeling overwhelmed.

In Part I, we discussed the value of being grounded in purpose and aligning your mission with your leadership role. This rudder will steady you amidst the storms of executive responsibility. With these stabilizing frameworks, it becomes easier to assess the landscape, gain insights into the intricacies of your new role, clarify your mandate, and craft a vision that inspires and guides.

In Part II, we delved into the heart of leadership—your team. We explored how to deepen their connection to purpose, transforming a group of individuals into a cohesive, motivated force. We focused on the culture that drives extraordinary success and principles for upgrading your team, strategically selecting and refining talents, and fostering collaboration that transcends the ordinary.

In Part III, we took the theory and turned it into actionable plans and systems. This included architecting your role, defining responsibilities and priorities, and setting the stage for impactful leadership. When developing the team action plan, we translated a mission into actionable steps, unleashing your team's collective power. Lastly, we discussed principles for wiring in continuous improvement, recognizing that there will be ongoing evolution, requiring growth, adaptability, and a commitment to excellence.

As you step into (or back into) your leadership position, we hope you will embrace all that it means to be a purpose-driven leader, delivering extraordinary results and empowering teams that thrive. Your role as an executive is not just a position; it's an opportunity to make a lasting impact, leaving an indelible mark on your team and organization.

Thank you for accompanying us on this odyssey of leadership. May your purpose be clear, your vision be compelling, and your journey be filled with triumphs that resonate far beyond the confines of your executive role. The adventure of purposeful leadership continues, and the world eagerly awaits the impact of your leadership legacy. Safe travels.

We hope this book has provided valuable insights for your leadership journey.

Ad Lucem (to the light)...

APPENDIX

Supplemental Chapter Resources

Visit **BeAnIntentionalExecutive.com** to download a free PDF copy of these Appendix exercises.

1A: Articulate Your Core Values

Take a few moments to (re)consider your core values for yourself, your team, and/or your organization as applicable.

We suggest limiting them to no more than five. This is not to suggest you can't have more than five values, but focus on the top five values that you most want to define who you are. Any more than this, you will diminish their stickiness and ability to remember them.

Once you've completed this first pass, take a few moments to write a clarifying statement of a few sentences that clearly illustrate what each of these values means. These descriptions should provide clarity on what matters most.

We encourage you not to edit them as you write the first time. Relatedly, if you have more than five values listed on your first pass, that's okay. You can prioritize or rework them as necessary. Allow yourself to think freely on your first pass. Then, after you've got a first draft, iterate on them as appropriate (with the questions below as guides).

Core Value #1: _____

What does this mean to you?:

Core Value #2: _____

What does this mean to you?:

Core Value #3: _____

What does this mean to you?:

Core Value #4: _____

What does this mean to you?:

Core Value #5: _____

What does this mean to you?:

As you review what you have written, ask yourself the following:

1. Do they clearly answer the question, what do you want to be known for?

2. Are they articulated in the affirmative? (i.e., they do not contain "shalt not" statements)

3. Are these your highest priority values? (recommend not more than 5)

4. Do they genuinely reflect who you are or can reasonably be? (It's okay to be aspirational, but they shouldn't be detached from reality.)

5. Are they sticky? Do they have a short, interesting, memorable phrase of not more than a few words for each?

1B: Your Personal Purpose Discovery Exercise

If you don't yet have an articulated personal purpose statement (or you are looking to revise your existing statement), here is a framework you can leverage to help you do so.

Part 1: Reflect on Your Story

- What experiences have shaped who you are?
- What challenges have you overcome?
- What patterns emerge in your successes?
- When have you felt most alive and engaged?
- What problems do you love solving?

Part 2: Identify Your Strengths

- What unique talents do you possess?
- What do others consistently praise you for?
- What comes naturally to you?
- When do you lose track of time?
- What expertise have you developed?

Part 3: Understand Your Impact

- How do you create value for others?
- What problems do you solve well?
- When have you made the most significant difference?
- What needs do you see in the world?
- How could your talents address these needs?

Part 4: Envision Your Legacy

- What mark do you want to leave?
- How do you want to be remembered?
- What change do you want to create?
- Who do you want to impact?
- What would make your life meaningful?

Part 5: Synthesize Your Purpose Using your reflections above:

1. List 3-5 themes that emerge
2. Identify connections between themes
3. Draft several purpose statements using the format: "I exist to* [action] [recipient] to [impact]" (*alternate framing options include: "My purpose is to...", "I am driven to...", "I create value by...", "I serve others through...", "My work enables...")
4. Refine your statement until it resonates deeply
5. Test it by asking:
    - Does this inspire me?
    - Is it authentic to who I am?
    - Does it serve others?
    - Can I build my life around it?
    - Will it sustain me long-term?

Remember: Your purpose statement should be:

- Clear and concise
- Action-oriented
- Focused on impact
- Authentic to you
- Inspiring to others

Example Personal Purpose Statements:

- "My purpose is to develop leaders who transform their organizations."
- "I create value by bridging technology and human needs."
- "I serve others through unlocking their potential."
- "My work enables communities to thrive through sustainable innovation."

Moving From Purpose to Vision

Now that you've crafted and tested your purpose statement, you're ready to translate it into an actionable vision that brings your purpose to life. At the same time, purpose is your enduring 'why,' vision is your concrete picture of 'what' you will create, and 'how' you will achieve it.

1. Near-term Impact (1-2 years)
- How will you manifest your purpose in your current role?
- What specific impact do you aim to create?
- How will you develop yourself and others?

2. Future Direction (3-5 years)
- How do you see your leadership evolving?
- What capabilities will you build?
- What legacy do you want to create?

3. Vision Statement Development: Draft several vision statements using: 'I will create/build/develop [what] by [how] to achieve [impact].'

Test your vision statement against these criteria:

- Does it align with your purpose?
- Is it both ambitious and achievable?

- Does it inspire action?
- Can others connect with it?
- Will it guide daily decisions?

1C: Organizational Purpose Discovery Exercise

If you don't yet have an articulated organizational purpose statement (or are looking to revise your existing statement), here is a framework you can leverage to help you and your team do so.

Part 1: Examine Your Origins & Evolution

- Why was the organization founded?
- What problems were you created to solve?
- How has your mission evolved?
- What consistent themes emerge?
- What values have endured?

Part 2: Assess Your Impact

- Who do you serve?
- What unique value do you deliver?
- What would be lost if you disappeared?
- Where do you make the most significant difference?
- What capabilities set you apart?

Part 3: Understand Your Stakeholders

- Who depends on your success?
- What do they value most?
- How do you improve their lives?
- What needs are unmet?
- Where could you create more value?

Part 4: Connect Individual & Organizational Purpose

- How do individual purposes align with organizational goals?
- Where do personal values intersect with company values?
- What shared aspirations exist?
- How can individual strengths serve organizational needs?
- What collective impact is possible?

Part 5: Craft Your Purpose Statement Using your insights above:

1. Identify key themes across all dimensions
2. Draft purpose statements using the format: "We exist to [action] [recipient] to [impact]."
3. Test each statement against these criteria:
   - Does it inspire employees?
   - Does it serve stakeholders?
   - Is it authentic to capabilities?
   - Can it drive sustainable success?
   - Will it endure over time?
   - Does it connect to individual purposes?

Part 6: Align & Activate

1. Map how your purpose:
   - Guides strategy
   - Shapes culture
   - Influences decisions
   - Drives behavior
   - Measures success
2. Create an activation plan:
   - Communication strategy

- Leadership alignment
- Employee engagement
- Performance metrics
- Recognition systems

Example Organizational Purpose Statements (from company websites and official annual reports 2023-2024):

1. Patagonia: "We're in business to save our home planet"
2. IKEA: "To create a better everyday life for the many people"
3. Unilever: "To make sustainable living commonplace"
4. Microsoft: "To empower every person and every organization on the planet to achieve more"
5. Disney: "To entertain, inform and inspire people around the globe through the power of unparalleled storytelling"
6. Nike: "To bring inspiration and innovation to every athlete* in the world" (*If you have a body, you are an athlete)
7. Starbucks: "To inspire and nurture the human spirit – one person, one cup and one neighborhood at a time"
8. CVS Health: "Helping people on their path to better health"
9. LinkedIn: "To connect the world's professionals to make them more productive and successful"

Remember, strong organizational purposes:

- Connect to individual purposes
- Guide strategic choices
- Inspire stakeholders
- Drive sustainable performance
- Create a meaningful impact
- Endure over time

This framework provided above can help your organization (re)discover and articulate your purpose while ensuring it connects meaningfully to individual team members' purposes and drives sustainable value creation.[252 253 254 255 256 257 258]

Translating Purpose into Vision

With your organizational purpose definitively articulated and tested, the next step is creating a vision that transforms this purpose into an actionable direction. Your purpose serves as the foundation and guiding star, while your vision provides the concrete picture of how you'll manifest that purpose in the coming years.

1. Near-term Direction (1-2 years)
   - How will we manifest our purpose?
   - What specific outcomes will we create?
   - How will we engage and develop our team?
2. Future Impact (3-5 years)
   - How will we evolve our capabilities?
   - What market position will we occupy?
   - What organizational legacy will we build?
3. Vision Alignment - Ensure your vision:
   - Clearly connects to purpose
   - Engages stakeholders
   - Guides strategic choices
   - Enables meaningful work
   - Drives sustainable success
4. Vision Statement Development - Create vision statements that:
   - Build on purpose
   - Inspire action

- Guide decisions
- Enable measurement
- Support communication

Test your vision through these lenses:

- Stakeholder value
- Team engagement
- Market differentiation
- Operational feasibility
- Cultural alignment

2A: Listening Tour Questions

We have provided the following questions as thought starters as you draft those you want to use for your listening tour. You should adapt these as you deem appropriate for your context. The goal is not to complete this list rotely.

These are ultimately intended to be good conversation starters, and they will undoubtedly uncover areas in which you can ask appropriate follow-up questions.

We encourage you to start with appreciative/affirmative questions to prime the pump for more generative thinking. This strengths-based approach leads to more inclusive engagement and innovative solutions by inviting people to be part of creating the future.

People who focus on strengths and possibilities feel more empowered to contribute to solutions. While problem-focused questions often surface already-known issues, appreciative questions help uncover opportunities and pathways forward.

High-level questions

- What has this organization accomplished in recent years that is new and noteworthy? Have we communicated it widely and taken full advantage of it?
- What is the organization's most significant strategic opportunity?
- Can you describe the company's biggest market problem in one sentence?
- What do customers/partners/suppliers think about the company? Has that changed?

- What one thing (if we could change it) would significantly impact our future?

Big Picture

- How do we uniquely serve our customers?
- What do our customers value most from our organization?
- What are the key drivers impacting the business?
- What are the strengths that we could be leveraging better?
- How would you define our most significant challenge in one sentence?

Operations

- How is the overall operational performance, and which way is it trending?
- Where are the areas of strength and opportunity in our operations?
- What has this organization accomplished recently that has improved performance?
- What can be done to run the business better or be more efficient?

The Individual, Team, and Department

- What do you / the team / the department do best?
- If you could pick one thing to change that would make your job easier or allow you to accomplish more, what would that be?
- What do we need to improve upon? What are potential landmines?
- Are there any other key internal stakeholder needs or dynamics that I should be aware of from your perspective?

Customers - Customer experience

- Describe a positive experience you have had with us, either in terms of using our products/services and/or any interactions you have had with us.
- What was it about this experience that you most appreciated/ valued?
- What is the most critical need we can help you meet? What drew you to this product/service/us as a company? What keeps you using our products/services?
- How likely are you to refer our products/services/us to a friend? Why?
- What might we do to serve you even better?
- Is there anything else you would like to share with me?

Additional Ideas

- How does X work?
- Why is it done that way?
- What's working well?
- What would it look like for this to work perfectly, beyond your wildest expectations?
- Where is the most growth potential? For innovation?
- What are we really good at, better than anyone else?
- When things are working perfectly around here, what is happening regarding how people work together?
- What are your top priorities?
- Where should we start?
- What do you want? Why?

2B: Due Diligence Checklist

The following list (not necessarily exhaustive) represents a potential list of collateral that will be helpful as you get to know your business context. The example below is for tech-driven global public companies, but you will want to customize it based on your functional responsibilities and industry.

Title	Category	Description
Strategy	Corporate Organization	copies of all written strategic documents, both internal and external, including analyst calls, partner communications, and product plans and roadmaps
Budgets	Accounting	copies of all budgets and operating plans prepared for at least the next 12 months
Financial Statements - Audited	Accounting	copies of audited financial statements for the past 2 completed fiscal years
Projections	Accounting	copies of relevant financial projections prepared for at least the next 12 months
Pricing Policies	Commercial Policies	copies of policies and procedures related to pricing
Product Testing Policies	Commercial Policies	summary of policies and practices related to product testing, including the results of any such tests

Joint Ventures	Corporate Organization	summary of joint venture agreements, partnership agreements, or agreements involving the sharing of profits, technology, marketing, or distribution efforts
Organizational Chart	Corporate Organization	organizational chart showing the corporate structure and all subsidiaries and affiliates
Customer List	Customers	a list of the top 25 customers for the past 2 years, including revenue
Customer Terminations	Customers	a list of all material customers that have ceased doing business with the company in the past 12 months, including a description of the circumstances surrounding the termination of any such relationship
Sales Channel List	Customers	a list of all material sales channel partners for each of the past 2 years, including revenue (e.g., sales reps and/or distributors)
Sales Data	Customers	a breakdown of sales and gross profits by: product type, geography, and sales channel
Org Charts / Headcount	General HR	organizational chart and headcount by function and location that will be within your purview
Enterprise Architecture	GRC/Enterprise Architect	description of your business model with interconnections to critical

		business functions, units, and data required to operate
GDPR Internal Assessments	GRC/IT Administration	processes for conducting internal and routine GDPR assessments to meet IOC reporting requirements
GDPR External Audits	GRC/IT Administration	all audit findings to include remediation and /or compensating controls
Corporate Risk Strategy	GRC	description of how the company assesses, categorizes, and manages risks
Corporate Risk Appetite Statement	GRC	description of which and how much risk executive leadership is willing to tolerate by business area
Jointly-Owned IP	IP Contracts	summary of any IP that is not solely owned (e.g., joint ownership, non-exclusive license, etc.)
Licensing Agreements	IP Contracts	summary of any relevant licensing agreements to or from 3rd parties for use of or by any licensed IP
IP Development	IP Development	summary of the process for generating/developing, recognizing, capturing, and protecting (for instance, via patents) IP assets

2C: Purpose-Aligned Strategic Assessment Framework

This framework helps you evaluate opportunities and challenges through a purpose-driven lens, ensuring strategic decisions support sustainable value creation while maintaining organizational authenticity.

1. Purpose Alignment

Evaluate how well opportunities align with your purpose:

- How does this serve our core purpose?
- Does it authentically reflect our values?
- Will it strengthen our culture?
- Does it enable meaningful work?
- How does it create value for stakeholders?

2. Capability Assessment

Consider your organization's ability to deliver:

Current Strengths

- What unique capabilities can we leverage?
- Where do we consistently excel?
- What cultural assets support this?

Development Needs

- What capabilities must we build?
- Where do we need to grow?

- What support systems are required?

3. Impact Evaluation

Assess potential outcomes across key dimensions:

Stakeholder Value

- Customer impact
- Team member growth
- Community benefit
- Business sustainability

Resource Requirements

- Time investment
- Financial needs
- People requirements
- Cultural implications

4. Implementation Readiness

Rate each initiative (1-5 scale):
- Purpose alignment
- Capability match
- Resource availability
- Team readiness
- Stakeholder support

5. Action Planning Template

Initiative Overview:
- Purpose connection
- Key stakeholders
- Success metrics
- Timeline

Critical Success Factors:
- Required capabilities:
- Resource needs:
- Support systems:
- Risk mitigations:

Implementation Steps:
1. Quick wins (30 days)
2. Building blocks (90 days)
3. Major milestones (6-12 months)

Guiding Questions:
- How does this advance our purpose?
- What capabilities do we need to build?
- How will we measure success?
- Who needs to be involved?
- What support systems are required?

Using This Framework:
1. Start with purpose alignment - if an initiative doesn't serve your core purpose, reconsider its priority
2. Be honest about capabilities - build what you need before launching major initiatives

3. Consider holistic impact - look beyond financial metrics
4. Plan realistically - better to do fewer things well
5. Review regularly - adjust as you learn and grow

Remember: This framework should support decision-making, not constrain it. Use it flexibly to ensure your strategic choices advance your purpose while building sustainable success.

2D: Strategic Relationship Tracker

Use this dashboard to track and strengthen key relationships across your network systematically. Regular updates help maintain meaningful connections and identify opportunities for deeper engagement while ensuring no important relationships fall through the cracks.

Name/ Role	What They Bring	What They Need	Current Status	Meeting Rhythm	Communication Preferences	Priority Actions	Last Review
[Example: CFO]	Financial expertise, Board connection	Strategic input, Tech updates	Strong/ Growing	Monthly 1:1, Quarterly review	Early morning calls, Brief emails	Share Q2 projections, Invite to tech review	3/15/25
[Example: Key Client]	Market insight, Revenue	Product roadmap clarity	Needs attention	Bi-weekly check-in	Video calls, Written follow-up	Schedule strategy sessions, Share new features	3/1/25

Implementation Guidelines:

1. Update quarterly or when significant changes occur
2. Focus on actionable insights
3. Keep entries brief but specific
4. Note both formal and informal interactions
5. Track patterns to optimize engagement

3A: Create your Teachable Point of View

Take a moment to capture what makes you the **perfect** leader for this moment.

Self-inventory

Begin with a quick self-inventory using the 5x5 approach we describe below. In bodybuilding, the 5x5 technique is supposed to build strength, grow muscles, and break plateaus. Similarly, a leadership 5x5 leans into your strengths in ways that drive organizational performance. Here's how it works: Ask yourself the following five questions, capturing 5 answers for each.

What is unique about my:

1. Capabilities: What unrivaled capabilities do I possess?
2. Knowledge: What specialized knowledge do I hold?
3. Experience: What extraordinary experiences have I had?
4. Perspective: What novel perspective do I bring?
5. Approach: What specialized approaches to problem solving and work do I have?

Capabilities	Knowledge	Experience	Perspective	Approach

Teachable Point of View

Once you have this 5x5 list:

- Identify the top 5 standout items on this list that you believe make you extraordinary, particularly for this role.
- Then, consider how those five things can be combined and work together to create unparalleled leadership in this role.
- Now, distill those into a single 2-3 sentence statement that summarizes what you bring to bear in this role, which will be the strength from which you lead.

  This 2-3 sentence statement is your **Teachable Point of View.**

3B: Create Your Transformation Plan

First 90 Day Goals:

Create your high-level plan, beginning with the major categories you must accomplish. We often start with the following categories and articulate what's in each:

1. **Deliver your day job:** This is your team's contribution to business as usual. In finance, this means closing the books every month; in Sales, it means meeting target revenue goals; and in manufacturing, it means meeting quality and production goals.

2. **Quick wins:** You do not have the luxury of waiting three months to demonstrate your value. Take the opportunity to build a reputation with short-term wins that matter to the company.

3. **Systems:** Develop a system (put a process in place) that ensures you meet all your stated goals while keeping you and your team at the top of your game. These are the set of actions and processes that automate keeping the trains on the tracks, enable your success, and ensure you continue to improve.

4. **Bigger wins:** Put longer-term goals in place and undertake the tasks that will set you and your team up to deliver on these bigger goals, or big, hairy, audacious goals (BHAGs).[259]

	First 90-Day Goals
Day Job	
Quick wins	
Systems	
Bigger wins	

Month-by-Month Plan:

This is the basic construct for a good first three months, with a starting point for priorities and focus areas that we have found to work for most executives. The following are good starting points for the activities you want to undertake in your first three months.

Month 1: Know the org

- Deep dives with the team, key partners, and leadership to gain a solid understanding of the unique value-add
- Confirm focus, priorities, partners, and rhythms
- Understand key drivers impacting the organization and areas of opportunity, both internal and external

Month 2: Build connections and identify opportunities

- Align team, optimize rhythms, engage partners
- Optimize priorities, rhythms, and build key relationships
- Align expectations, identify early wins

Month 3: Deliver the mandate

- Agree (and refine) the mandate with the manager, peers, and team
- Build "guiding principles" that resonate
- Identify opportunities that will drive value
- Capture early wins that build momentum and catalyze transformation
- Map out critical strategy, people, process, and technology shifts
- Architect the transformation agenda and gain alignment

4A: Brainstorming rules

Borrowing a page from the IDEO design firm and setting up key ground rules that they identify below will help enable this process.[260]

1 — Defer Judgment
Creative spaces are judgment-free zones—they let ideas flow so people can build from each other's great ideas.

2 — Encourage Wild Ideas
Embrace the most out-of-the-box notions. There's often not a whole lot of difference between outrageous and brilliant.

3 — Build on the Ideas of Others
Try using "and" instead of "but." It encourages positivity and inclusivity and leads to many ideas.

4 — Stay Focused on the Topic
Try to keep the discussion on target. Divergence is good, but you must keep your eyes on the prize.

5 — One Conversation at a Time
This can be difficult—especially with many creative people in a single room—but always consider the challenge topic and how to stay on track.

6 — Be Visual
Use colored markers and Post-its. Stick your ideas on the wall so others can visualize them.

7 — Go for Quantity
Crank your ideas out quickly. For any 60-minute session, you should seek to generate 100 ideas.

4B: Purpose-Driven Team Exercises

Introduction

These exercises provide practical tools for implementing the purpose-driven leadership concepts discussed in Chapter 4. They are designed to help teams connect theory to practice, driving engagement and performance through meaningful work.

Each exercise includes detailed instructions, timing guidelines, and implementation tips. While comprehensive, they should be adapted to your specific context and culture. Start with what resonates most for your team, gather feedback, adjust as needed, and build on success to create momentum.

Exercise 1: Purpose Discovery Workshop

Time needed: 2-3 hours
Participants: Full team

Exercise Structure:

a) Individual Reflection (20 minutes)
Have each participant reflect on and write answers to:
- What attracted you to this organization?
- When have you felt most proud of our work?
- What impact do we create for others?
- What unique value do we deliver?

b) Small Group Discussion (40 minutes)
Break into groups of 4-5 people to:
- Share individual stories
- Identify common themes

- Capture key insights
- Draft purpose statements

c) Full Team Integration (60 minutes)

Bring the whole team together to:

- Share key themes from each group
- Identify overlapping elements
- Draft collective purpose statements
- Test against the current work

Exercise 2: Purpose-Impact Mapping

Time needed: 90 minutes

Participants: Team leads or the entire team

Exercise Structure:

a) Map Current Activities (30 minutes)

Create a visual showing:

- Key activities/projects
- Target outcomes
- Customer impact
- Business value

b) Purpose Alignment Check (30 minutes)

For each activity, assess:

- How does this serve our purpose?
- What value does it create?
- Should we do more/less?
- What's missing?

c) Action Planning (30 minutes)

- Identify alignment gaps
- Prioritize changes needed

- Create action plans
- Assign ownership

Exercise 3: Customer Impact Stories

Time needed: 60 minutes

Participants: Full team

Exercise Structure:

a) Story Collection (20 minutes)

Each team member shares:

- A specific customer interaction
- The problem solved
- The impact created
- The lesson learned

b) Theme Analysis (20 minutes)

Collectively identify:

- Common elements
- Unique value delivered
- Purpose connections
- Improvement opportunities

c) Application Planning (20 minutes)

Develop plans for:

- Creating more impact
- Sharing stories systematically
- Improving processes
- Recognizing contributions

Implementation Guidelines

1. Preparation
- Choose appropriate timing
- Secure necessary resources
- Prepare materials
- Brief participants
- Set clear objectives

2. Facilitation Tips
- Create psychological safety
- Encourage full participation
- Manage time effectively
- Capture key insights
- Drive to action

3. Follow-through
- Document outcomes
- Assign ownership
- Schedule check-ins
- Track progress
- Celebrate wins

Measuring Success

Track both quantitative and qualitative metrics:

1. Engagement Indicators
- Employee satisfaction scores
- Participation rates
- Voluntary turnover
- Absenteeism rates

2. Performance Metrics

- Productivity measures
- Quality indicators
- Customer satisfaction
- Innovation metrics

3. Cultural Indicators

- Purpose alignment scores
- Team collaboration
- Knowledge sharing
- Change adoption

4. Business Impact

- Customer retention
- Revenue growth
- Profitability
- Market share

Implementation Timeline

Week 1-2:

- Select an appropriate exercise
- Prepare materials
- Schedule a session
- Brief participants

Week 3-4:

- Conduct an exercise
- Document outcomes
- Create action plans
- Assign ownership

Week 5-8:

- Implement changes
- Track progress
- Gather feedback
- Make adjustments

Week 9-12:

- Measure impact
- Share success stories
- Plan the next steps
- Scale what works

Note: These exercises should be adapted to your context, team size, and organizational culture. Start with what resonates most for your team and build from there.

Citations:

- Quinn, R. E., & Thakor, A. V. (2019). *The economics of higher purpose: Eight counterintuitive steps for creating a purpose-driven organization.* Berrett-Koehler Publishers.
- Gartenberg, C., Prat, A., & Serafeim, G. (2019). *Corporate purpose and financial performance. Organization Science, 30(1),* 1-18.
- Mackey, J., & Sisodia, R. (2014). *Conscious capitalism: Liberating the heroic spirit of business.* Harvard Business Review Press.

5A: Reflect on What Makes Your Work Meaningful

Reflecting on the core elements of *Lips-Wiersma's Map of Meaningful Work[261] will give you a sense of areas to emphasize and identify gaps you may be experiencing that desire more attention. Mindfully consider and jot down your thoughts on the following questions:

- What inspires you in your life and for your work?
- What things support a sense of integrity with self in your work?
- What makes you feel like you can express your full potential in your work?
- What aspects of your work fulfill the need to serve others?
- What elements create a sense of unity with others?

While these elements of meaningful work can provide valuable insights for your team, it's essential to approach this exploration with sensitivity and respect for individual boundaries. This reflection should be offered by invitation rather than mandate—team members should feel free to engage at their comfort level.

Some may wish to keep their sources of meaning private, while others may be eager to share. As a leader, your role is to create space for this discussion while respecting that each person's journey to meaningful work is personal.

- What inspires your team members in their lives and at work?
- What do those things support a sense of integrity with self in their work?

- What makes them feel like they can express their full potential in their work?
- What aspects of their work fulfill the need to serve others?
- What elements create a sense of unity with others?

What broader insights do these reflections yield? Can you nurture how you find meaning as a group and create a shared sense of meaning and purpose?

What actions can you take to enhance these insights for yourself and/or for your team?

*Lips-Wiersma establishes these definitions for four key pathways to meaningful work:

Integrity with Self: Being true to your authentic self while growing and developing through your work and life experiences. This includes developing critical inner qualities like confidence, wisdom, patience, and moral courage that allow you to stay aligned with your values.

Unity with Others: The deep sense of fulfillment from genuine human connection and collaboration. This includes the satisfaction of achieving goals as a team, feeling like you truly belong, and experiencing deep mutual understanding with others.

Expressing Full Potential: The satisfaction of making your unique contribution and achieving meaningful accomplishments. It is about meeting our human need to create value and impact, whether through innovation, service excellence, or other achievements that utilize our distinct capabilities.

Service to Others: The sense of purpose derived from making a positive difference in the lives of others. This could be through supporting colleagues, delivering value to customers, contributing to your community, or working toward broader societal or environmental benefits.

5B: Creating Your Leadership User Manual

Purpose: A leadership user manual is a tool for making your working preferences, communication style, and ways of thinking explicit. It helps others understand how to work with you effectively while building trust through transparency. This guide provides a framework for creating your user manual and implementing this practice with your team.

Suggested Components

Your user manual can address the following:

1. Working Style
   - When I'm at my best (time of day, conditions)
   - How I prefer to receive information
   - My decision-making approach
   - How do I handle stress/pressure
   - What energizes/drains me

2. Communication Preferences
   - The best ways to reach me
   - Meeting preferences
   - Feedback style (giving and receiving)
   - How to disagree with me
   - What I value in discussions

3. Values and Priorities
   - What I value most in teammates
   - My non-negotiables
   - What motivates me

- My definition of success
- My blind spots

4. Support Needs
- How to help me when I'm stressed
- Signs that I'm overwhelmed
- The best ways to challenge my thinking
- What I need in critical situations

Sample Template:

About Me
- My leadership philosophy is...
- I thrive when...
- I struggle when...

How to Work With Me
- The best way to communicate with me is...
- I prefer meetings that are...
- When you need my input, please...
- When you disagree with me, I'd like you to...

What I Value
- I appreciate people who...
- I get frustrated by...
- You can count on me to...
- I want to be better at...

Implementation Guidelines:

1. Start with Leadership
- Create your manual first

- Share it with your team
- Explain the benefits and purpose
- Invite questions and discussion

2. Extend to Team
- Make participation voluntary
- Provide a template, but allow customization
- Create sharing opportunities
- Update periodically

3. Use Effectively
- Reference in onboarding
- Use in team development
- Revisit during conflicts
- Update as needed

Example Excerpts:
- "I'm a morning person and do my best strategic thinking before noon. I prefer to handle complex decisions and creative work early in the day, saving operational discussions for afternoons."
- "I value direct communication. If you disagree with me, please tell me directly rather than hinting. I promise to listen without judgment and appreciate the courage to speak up."
- "When stressed, I tend to become quieter and focused. This isn't personal - I just need time to process it. The best way to help is to give me space while staying available if I need to talk things through."

Additional Resources:
- The Making of a Manager by Julie Zhuo
- Think Again by Adam Grant

- First, Break All the Rules by Marcus Buckingham
- The Culture Code by Daniel Coyle

Remember: User manuals should be living documents that evolve as you learn and grow. They facilitate understanding and communication, not create rigid rules or expectations. Participants should be granted agency regarding how much information and in what manner they feel comfortable sharing.

6A: Assess Your Cultural Foundation and Opportunities

This framework helps you evaluate how well your actions and systems support your desired culture. The assessment process involves three key steps:

STEP 1: Review Your Values

1. List your articulated organizational values:
- Value 1:
- Value 2:
- Value 3:
- Value 4:
- Value 5:

2. Identify values demonstrated in your "high point" stories:
- Story 1:
- Key values demonstrated:
- Story 2:
- Key values demonstrated:

3. Note any gaps between stated and demonstrated values:
- Gaps identified:
- Potential reasons:
- Areas for alignment:

STEP 2: Evaluate Cultural Elements for each of the six elements discussed in Chapter 6, rate current status (1-5) and gather evidence:

Psychological Safety
- Observable behaviors that support/hinder:
- Team member feedback:
- Meeting dynamics:
- Response to mistakes: Rating: ____ Evidence: ____

Performance Excellence
- Standards demonstrated:
- Achievement recognition:
- Improvement processes:
- Team engagement: Rating: ____ Evidence: ____

Operational Autonomy
- Decision-making levels:
- Resource control:
- Process flexibility:
- Innovation support: Rating: ____ Evidence: ____

Growth Focus
- Development opportunities:
- Learning from mistakes:
- Feedback processes:
- Innovation encouragement: Rating: ____ Evidence: ____

Kinship
- Team connections:
- Collaboration patterns:
- Support behaviors:

- Community building: Rating: ___ Evidence: ___

Abundance Mindset
- Problem-solving approach:
- Resource sharing:
- Growth orientation:
- Possibility thinking: Rating: ___ Evidence: ___

STEP 3: Assess Cultural Levers

Leadership Actions

Current Practice	Supports Culture	Needs Change	Next Steps
Decision-making approach			
Handling of mistakes			
Recognition practices			
Value demonstration			

People Practices

Current Practice	Supports Culture	Needs Change	Next Steps
Hiring/promotion criteria			
Development approaches			
Feedback methods			

Celebration practices			

Operational Systems

Current Practice	Supports Culture	Needs Change	Next Steps
Meeting structures			
Information sharing			
Resource allocation			
Success measures			

Implementation Guidelines:

1. Gather Multiple Perspectives
   - Conduct informal interviews
   - Use anonymous surveys
   - Observe team interactions
   - Review employee feedback
   - Analyze exit interviews

2. Look for Patterns
   - What themes emerge?
   - Where do you see consistency?
   - Where do you notice gaps?
   - What surprises you?

3. Prioritize Actions
   - What changes would have the most significant impact?
   - What can be implemented quickly?
   - What requires a longer-term focus?
   - What needs additional resources?

4. Create an Action Plan For Each Priority Area:
- Specific changes needed
- Resources required
- Timeline for implementation
- Success measures
- Review schedule

5. Regular Review Schedule Quarterly Assessments to:
- Track progress
- Identify new opportunities
- Adjust approaches
- Celebrate successes
- Plan next actions

Remember:
- Culture is built through consistent actions
- Small changes can have significant impacts
- Focus on a few changes at a time
- Involve the team in improvement efforts
- Celebrate progress regularly

Sample Assessment Questions:
1. How do we typically respond when someone makes a mistake?
2. What behaviors do we actually reward?
3. How do we make important decisions?
4. What stories do we tell about our successes?
5. How do we handle disagreement?
6. What gets celebrated here?
7. How do we develop our people?
8. What behaviors get promoted?

This framework should be used as a living tool, regularly updated as you learn and grow. Use it to identify specific opportunities to strengthen your cultural foundation and create sustainable, positive change.

6B: Psychological Safety Assessment Questions

These reflection questions are designed to help leaders and teams evaluate psychological safety and identify opportunities for improvement. Consider using them in team discussions, one-on-one conversations, or personal reflection.

For Leaders:

1. How do you typically respond when someone brings you bad news?
2. What signals might you be sending that discourage speaking up?
3. Where do you see evidence of psychological safety in your team?
4. What barriers to psychological safety exist in your organization?
5. How do you model learning from mistakes?

For Teams:

1. What helps you feel safe speaking up?
2. When have you felt hesitant to share ideas?
3. How can we better support learning from mistakes?
4. What would make it easier to raise concerns?
5. How can we improve our feedback processes?

Implementation Guidelines:

- Consider an anonymous collection of responses for more candid feedback
- Discuss patterns rather than individual responses
- Focus on specific behaviors rather than general impressions
- Identify 1-2 concrete actions based on insights

- Schedule follow-up to assess progress

Remember that psychological safety is built through consistent actions over time. Regular assessment using these questions can help track progress and identify emerging challenges before they become significant barriers.

7A: Process Improvement: Is / Should Mapping

What is "is / should" mapping:

"Is" ("As is") map: The "is" map is a process flow and visual diagram that captures the current workflows as they exist today. It includes all steps, decision points, potential and recognized bottlenecks. It is typically messy, highlighting the areas where work or progress is stuck, rework is needed, and errors are made.

"Should" ("should be" or "to be") map: The "should" map outlines the improved process design based on analysis of the "as is" map, incorporating changes to eliminate inefficiencies, streamline activities, and achieve desired outcomes.

Why use "is / should" mapping:

"Is / Should" mapping is a practical method for identifying areas for high-impact improvements that facilitates clear communication and enables stakeholder buy-in. By comparing the current process ("is" map) with the ideal process ("should" map), you can quickly identify areas where improvements are needed to optimize efficiency and effectiveness. Visualizing current and desired states helps teams make informed decisions about which changes to prioritize and implement and better understand their impact.

7B: Sample Team Rhythms and Routines Framework

This framework provides a starting point for mapping your team's activities and ensuring they align with strategic goals. While every organization's needs will differ, this template illustrates common patterns we've observed in high-performing teams. Use it as a foundation to create your customized business rhythm that supports operational excellence and strategic advancement.

The framework is organized by time horizon (daily through annual) to help you balance immediate operational needs with longer-term strategic objectives. For each activity, consider:

- Purpose/Goal: What specific outcome does this routine support?
- Participants: Who needs to be involved?
- Outputs: What tangible deliverables should result?

Adapt these elements based on your team's context, culture, and objectives. The most effective routines become natural parts of your team's work rather than bureaucratic obligations.

Daily Routines:

Activity	Purpose/Goal	Participants	Outputs
15-min Stand-up	Align priorities, remove blockers	Core team	Action items, escalations
Metrics Review	Track key performance indicators	Team leads	Performance dashboard update
End-of-day Check-in	Ensure critical handoffs	Shift teams	Transition log

Weekly Routines:

Activity	Purpose/Goal	Participants	Outputs
Team Planning	Set weekly priorities, review progress	All team members	Weekly priorities, resource allocation
Cross-functional Sync	Coordinate dependencies	Partner teams	Integration plan updates
Customer Review	Track satisfaction metrics	Customer-facing teams	Customer health scorecard

Monthly Routines:

Activity	Purpose/Goal	Participants	Outputs
Strategic Review	Assess progress against goals	Leadership team	Strategy adjustments
Performance Review	Evaluate team metrics	Team leads	Performance improvement plans
Innovation Forum	Share new ideas/learnings	All teams	Innovation pipeline

Quarterly Routines:

Activity	Purpose/Goal	Participants	Outputs
OKR Planning	Set/adjust quarterly goals	All teams	Updated OKRs
Talent Review	Assess development needs	Leadership	Development plans
Business Review	Evaluate financial performance	Executive team	Financial forecasts

Annual Routines:

Activity	Purpose/Goal	Participants	Outputs
Strategic Planning	Set annual objectives	All stakeholders	Annual plan
Team Offsite	Build team alignment	All team members	Team charter update
Capability Assessment	Evaluate team strengths/gaps	Leadership	Capability roadmap

8A: Framework for Structuring Your Time

Mary's Matrix

While this framework seems simple, its power as a tool to ensure that your network stays healthy and that you can make and maintain the connections you need to lead effectively is unparalleled. We encourage you to set your plan for these touchpoints, schedule them at the beginning of the year, and update it quarterly (or anytime you take on a new role).

Stakeholders	Weekly	Bi-weekly	Monthly	Bi-Monthly	Quarterly
Team / Direct Reports	Name, Schedule Name, Schedule Name, Schedule ...				
Core Stakeholders					
Cross- Functional Allies					
Mentors / Mentees					
Other Internal Connections					
External Network					
Conferences / Events					

9A: High-Level Framework for Planning an Appreciative Inquiry Summit

This framework provides a high-level guide for organizing and executing an Appreciative Inquiry Summit, a powerful tool for engaging large groups in collaborative change. Based on the principles outlined in "The Appreciative Inquiry Summit: A Practitioner's Guide for Leading Large-Group Change" by James Lucema, Diana Whitney, Bernard Mohr, and Thomas Griffin. This approach focuses on leveraging organizational strengths and fostering a shared vision for the future.

1. Pre-Summit Planning:

- Define Purpose and Objectives: Clearly articulate the summit's purpose and desired outcomes. Engage stakeholders early to ensure alignment and buy-in.
- Identify Stakeholders: To obtain multiple perspectives, involve a diverse group of participants, including internal team members, external partners, and other relevant stakeholders.
- Logistics and Resources: Plan the logistics, including venue, technology needs, and materials. Ensure adequate resources and support for effective facilitation.
- Communication Strategy: Develop a communication plan to inform participants about the summit's purpose, agenda, and their role in the process.

2. Summit Structure:

- Opening Activities: Set a positive tone and build community with icebreakers, storytelling, or sharing success stories.

- Discovery Sessions: Facilitate sessions to explore and share organizational strengths and successes through storytelling and appreciative interviews.
- Vision Creation: Guide participants in envisioning a desired future for the organization, encouraging creative thinking and collaboration.
- Action Planning: Transition from visioning to action by identifying specific initiatives and projects. Assign roles and responsibilities to ensure accountability.

3. Post-Summit Implementation:

- Follow-Up Processes: Establish ongoing communication and follow-up mechanisms, including regular check-ins and progress reports.
- Accountability Measures: Set up systems to track progress and hold participants accountable for their commitments using metrics and milestones.
- Progress Tracking: Monitor the implementation of action plans, celebrate successes, and learn from challenges.
- Communication Plans: To maintain momentum, keep stakeholders informed about progress and outcomes by sharing stories of impact and success.

This framework is designed to help you harness your organization's collective wisdom and creativity, driving meaningful change through collaborative engagement.

10A: Reground on What Matters Most

If we are not careful, we can lose ourselves and dim the spark that made us so successful in the first place. We unwittingly discount our strengths and become some other, lesser version of ourselves. Take a few moments to reground yourself and what matters most to you.

As you consider these questions, pay attention to what other insights your heart, mind, and soul offer.

What do you want your legacy/impact to be at work and at home? What will people who matter to you say about what you have created and contributed to the communities of which you are a part?

Allow yourself to forecast this vision in full, vibrant, living color in your mind's eye. The more you can envision this for yourself, the more likely you will be able to manifest it in your thoughts, energies, and decisions along the way.

What are your core strengths and passions, and what are your weaknesses or blind spots? How will you build an appropriate support structure around your selected path?

Jot down your initial thoughts, then spend some more time later on how to action-plan around these particular areas.

Are there skill gaps you may need help with to succeed? What action steps might you take to identify these and develop a plan?

Reflecting on these identified strengths and gaps, consider what opportunities exist to leverage or shore these up more fully. Rough out a short-term (e.g., 90-day) and more extended-term (e.g., 12-18 months and 2-3 year visions).

10B: Framework for Structuring your time

Framework to Structure Thinking | Time

This framework helps leaders compartmentalize and balance near- and long-term considerations while maintaining stakeholder alignment. Below, we've included an anonymized example from one of our executive transition clients to illustrate how this framework can be applied in practice. Use these examples as inspiration while adapting the framework to your specific context.

Note: The following example is drawn from our work with a senior executive during their participation in our Executive Transition Boot Camp participation. While specific details have been modified to protect confidentiality, the structure and approach demonstrate how to use this framework effectively.

Leadership's ability to compartmentalize and continually balance near- and long-term considerations, take in new information, communicate effectively, and keep stakeholders aligned towards common objectives will be a key success factor going forward.

The following metaphoric framework will help shape thinking and identify actions. Additionally, it can be a useful tool that can be continually refreshed over time. Each area includes recommendations of actions to maintain/nurture, start or consider, and those to avoid.

1. Keep the Runway Clear: Contain & Delegate Urgent/Pressing Issues
2. Build the Rules for the Airways: Establish Timing, Cadence, Structure, and Processes

3. Communicate with the Control Tower: Ensure the Engage & Manage the Board
4. Establish the Flight Plan(s): Set the Vision & Strategy
5. Maintain On-time Flight Performance: Run the Business/ Programs

1. Keep the Runway Clear: Contain & Delegate Urgent/Pressing Issues

Nurture & Maintain	Start/Consider	Avoid
• An executive vantage point over the entirety of responsibilities • Using "Important/Urgent 2/2 matrix" to prioritize and triage big & small issues • Your "Monday Morning Cabinet Meetings" • Modeling a steady and thoughtful demeanor over a "whack-a-mole" or reactionary approach • Transparent two-way lines of communication with your team • A marathon pace with strategic sprints	• How can you consistently manage and communicate about issues within the broader context of the organization's vision, strategy, and values? • How can you build the triage capability and skill in others? Find opportunities to coach and lead. • Normalizing how the organization manages risks (e.g., controls, clear accountabilities, decision rights)	• Being "Chief Problem Solver" and letting issues get delegated up • Allowing one or a few issues to rule your time and energy • Trying to solve everything in one fell swoop • Escalating to the Board unless necessary • Over-engaging the Board for operational decisions within your purview • Getting mired in leadership performance

	• What formalities need to be introduced with your Cabinet? (e.g., how you assign and delegate; how you collaborate as a team) • What rubric will you use to ensure there are no surprises for the Board?	issues/moving indecisively when circumstances may call for more timely action
Add your own:		

2. Build the Rules for the Airways: Establish Timing, Cadence, Structure, and Processes

Nurture & Maintain	Start/Consider	Avoid
• Routine meetings and touchpoints with Board Officers, select Board Members, and Direct Reports	• Establish "top-down" rhythm to the organization • Orient the cadence of organizational decisions and actions to dial off Board meeting timing where possible	• Being reactionary and letting "bubble-up issues" take you off your game

• Standing meetings with your team • Skip level, town halls, and listening tour-type engagements • Orienting to important cycles (e.g., funding, planning, program, election) • Creating deadlines and milestones in years, quarters, and months.	• Where movement and action are necessary, like with agile software releases, think 1.0, 1.1, 2.0, etc., with an emphasis on progress and improvement, month over month, quarter over quarter, etc. • Roll out 1.0 of the new direct report structure, timed to the June Board meeting • Routine 1:1 meetings with your Direct Reports (e.g., monthly) • Fractional strategic communications leader to establish process and help develop content until a longer-term accountability and strategic communication plan is put in place • How will you measure the success of the organization, programs, and individuals? - Leverage what's working; put a plan in place for where development is needed	• Waiting for everything to be perfect. • Putting off difficult decisions, actions, and conversations
Add your own:		

3. Communicate with the Control Tower: Engage & Manage the Board

Nurture & Maintain	Start/Consider	Avoid
• Strong relationships with Officers and Board • Non-partisan, non-controversial wins (e.g., MWV-owned successes) • Board 1:1 Orientation touchpoints as high-impact conversations to influence and set expectations. • Exposing your team to the Board and vice versa	• Creating strong circle of Board advisors (including Officers and non-Officers) as sounding board and allies; even if informal • Influencing the process and encouraging Officers to pursue succession planning steps where possible • Informal keep-them-informed "non-Governance" updates to the Board (e.g., semi-monthly) between Board meetings • Assigning By-Law Cleanup to a staff member as a development assignment and exposure to the Board. Goal is to create alignment	• Asking Board for permission where they should just be informed • Surprises! • Sugar-coating • Only focusing on issues–be sure to balance communications with positive actions and results–if not you, then who will do this?

	between By-Laws and current operations • Identify product development and promotion plan and associated owner(s) for demonstrating program impact in sectors where traditional ag is challenged (e.g. minority/women-owned businesses, sustainable products)	
Add your own:		

4. Establish the Flight Plan(s): Set Vision & Strategy

Nurture & Maintain	Start/Consider	Avoid
• Set expectations and bound thinking with the Board and Leadership Team on anticipated funding bill possibilities, timing, and contingency plan.	• Develop your "answer key." (e.g., evolve your listening tour themes) • Share key elements of your vision and values informally and as part of the process (i.e., put	• Dictating • Pre-maturely halting discourse unless it is counter-productive • Letting this become "John's Vision" • Establishing disparate vision/process across the organizations

- Engagement from leadership team on the M,V,V process.
- Listening tour mindset with the rest of the organization - what is the next organic iteration?
- Keep the Board informed on process
- Be intentional about stakeholder involvement in the key pieces of this engagement for rapport building, vision alignment, and professional growth and development

your thumbprint on things)
- Be clear on what you consider bedrock
- Trust the process and create space for your people. Strategically pressure test where there may be deviations from your vision
- Balance process and substance in your engagements with the Board
- How can you deputize and build a "Justice League" approach from your leadership team?

- Pinning funding outcome to your tenure; at same time, minimizing the behind the scenes influence your organization and your lobbying efforts/educational leadership may have on the outcome itself,
- Creating a strategic plan without broader organizational buy-in/awareness that merely sits on a shelf

Add your own:

5. Maintain On-Time Flight Performance: Run the Business/Programs

Nurture & Maintain	Start/Consider	Avoid
• Delegation of CRM implementation for enhanced business development efforts • Strategic trade show engagement • Focus on effective/efficient on-boarding experiences	• Pick a "pet project" - this is the quick win this year... • Provide appropriate growth/leadership opportunities for your high-potentials (e.g., leading elements of the interviews, analysis, MVV work, etc.) • "C-Suite" leadership cabinet build-out plan and establishment of key MBO's for team • Prepare finance models and decision tree for alternate funding scenarios in the coming cycle, including key	• Ambiguous or imbalanced metrics / disjointed accountabilities • Redundancies/unnecessary complexity in cross-leadership structures (e.g., disparate communications leadership) • Disjointed promotion/restructuring efforts where they can be performed in concert • Relying solely on govt funding sources

	personnel components • Perform case study for business development; identify economic impact/revenue generation, connections, downstream impacts, etc. / leverage sustainability and equity efforts for competitive advantage	
Add your own:		

Additional Resources / Connect With Us

Thank you for joining us on this leadership journey. We hope this book has provided valuable insights for your path forward as a purpose-driven leader.

Visit BeAnIntentionalExecutive.com to download a free PDF copy of the Appendix exercises contained in this book.

For additional resources and support, visit adlucemgroup.com for:
- Leadership assessments
- Implementation tools
- Case studies
- Blog posts
- Newsletter

Additional Free Resources:
- Take our Leading for Peak Performance Assessment: adlucemgroup.com/additional-resources
- Schedule your free strategy assessment: https://adlucemgroup.com/get-started/

Leadership Development Programs:
- Executive Advisory Support
- Leadership Coaching
- Team Development
- Strategic Planning
- Culture Transformation
- Board Engagement

Your Next Strategic Move

If you're ready to put these leadership principles into immediate practice, we want to share something with you. Our *Succeed from Day One Executive Briefing* is a strategic accelerator that has helped hundreds of purpose-driven leaders navigate their critical first 90 days and beyond.

This is a practical briefing that includes:

- **Discover the 3 critical pitfalls that derail new executives** – and the evidence-based countermeasures that help you avoid them so you can accelerate your impact from day one.
- **Get 50 minutes of concentrated wisdom** from industry experts who've guided hundreds of successful leadership transitions, plus actionable frameworks you can implement immediately.
- **Access a complimentary one-on-one strategic session** with one of our executive leadership advisors to create your personalized roadmap for thriving in your new role.

Get instant access here: **https://adlucemgroup.com/succeed** or scan the QR code below.

Contact Us:
- Email: info@adlucemgroup.com
- Website: adlucemgroup.com

Let's Connect:

Follow us on LinkedIn:

https://www.linkedin.com/in/patrickfarran/
https://www.linkedin.com/in/melissanorcross/

Subscribe to our newsletter: https://adlucemgroup.com/blog/

Ad Lucem (to the light)...

Notes

[1] Keller, S., & Meaney, M. (2018). Successfully transitioning to new leadership roles. *McKinsey Quarterly*.

[2] SHRM. (n.d.). *Linking theory and practice in leadership transitions.* SHRM Executive Network. https://www.shrm.org/executive-network/insights/people-strategy/linking-theory-practice-leadership-transitions

[3] Burlingham, B. (2016). *Small Giants: Companies that choose to be great instead of big, 10th-anniversary edition.* Penguin.

[4] Hurst, A. (2014). *The Purpose Economy: How Your Desire for Impact, Personal Growth and Community Is Changing the World.* Elevate, a Russell Media company.

[5] Sisodia, R., Wolfe, D., & Sheth, J. (2007). *Firms of endearment: How world-class companies profit from passion and purpose.* Wharton School Publishing/Pearson Education.

[6] Askinosie, S., & Lawler, L. (2017). *Meaningful Work: A Quest to Do Great Business, Find Your Calling, and Feed Your Soul.* TarcherPerigee.

[7] Davis, W. (2005). *Creating a Culture of Excellence: Changing the World of Work One Person at a Time.* Authorhouse.

[8] George, B. (2007). *True north: Discover your authentic leadership.* John Wiley & Sons.

[9] Quinn, R. E., & Thakor, A. V. (2018). Creating a purpose-driven organization. *Harvard Business Review*, *96*(4), 78-85. https://hbr.org/2018/07/creating-a-purpose-driven-organization.

[10] FDIC (2022). USAA Federal Savings Bank FDIC Resolution Plan, retrieved from: *https://www.fdic.gov/resources/resolutions/resolution-authority/resplans/plans/usaa-idi-1807.pdf* and *https://www.fdic.gov/resources/resolutions/resolution-authority/resplans/plans/usaa-idi-2212.pdf* on 1 May 2023.

[11] FDIC (2022). USAA Federal Savings Bank FDIC Resolution Plan, retrieved from: *https://www.fdic.gov/resources/resolutions/resolution-authority/resplans/plans/usaa-idi-1807.pdf* on 1 May 2023.

[12]Quinn, R. E., & Thakor, A. V. (2018). Creating a purpose-driven organization. *Harvard Business Review, 96*(4), 78-85. https://hbr.org/2018/07/creating-a-purpose-driven-organization

[13] *Companies that care: Lessons from a unicorn founder and his purpose-driven investor. (May 11, 2022) McKinsey Digital. Downloaded April 14, 2024. https://www.mckinsey.com/business-functions/mckinsey-digital/our-insights/companies-that-care-lessons-from-a-unicorn-founder-and-his-purpose-driven-investor*

[14] Laloux, F. (2014), *Reinventing Organizations: A Guide to Creating Organizations Inspired by the Next Stage in Human Consciousness.* Nelson Parker.

[15] Sisodia, R., Wolfe, D., & Sheth, J. (2007). *Firms of endearment: How world-class companies profit from passion and purpose.* Wharton School Publishing/Pearson Education.

[16] Hurst, A. (2014). *The Purpose Economy: How Your Desire for Impact, Personal Growth and Community Is Changing the World.* Elevate, a Russell Media company.

[17] Mirshahzadeh, D. (2020) *The Core Value Equation: A framework to drive results, create limitless scale, and win the war for talent.* Lioncrest.

[18] Behn, R. D. (2003). Why measure performance? Different purposes require different measures. *Public administration review, 63(5), 586-606.*

[19] Ellsworth, R. R. (2002). *Leading with purpose: The new corporate realities.* Stanford University Press.

[20] Gartenberg, C., Prat, A., & Serafeim, G. (2019). Corporate purpose and financial performance. *Organization Science, 30(1), 1-18.*

[21] Gartenberg, C., Prat, A., & Serafeim, G. (2019). Corporate purpose and financial performance. *Organization Science, 30(1), 1-18.*

[22] Davis, W. (2005) *Creating a Culture of Excellence: Changing the World of Work One Person at a Time.* Authorhouse.

[23] Tichy, N. M. (2014). *Succession: Mastering the make or break process of leadership transition.* Penguin.

[24] Collins, J. C., & Porras, J. I. (2004). *Built to last: Successful habits of visionary companies.* Harper Business.

[25] George, B. (2003). Anne Mulcahy: Leading Xerox through the perfect storm. *Harvard Business School Case, 9-405-050.*

[26] Mulcahy, A. (2010). How I did it: Xerox's former CEO on why succession planning needs to start on day one. *Harvard Business Review, 88(10),* 47-51.

[27] Catmull, E., & Wallace, A. (2014). *Creativity, Inc.: Overcoming the unseen forces that stand in the way of true inspiration.* Random House.

[28] Lips-Wiersma, M., & Morris, L. (2018). *The Map of Meaningful Work: A practical guide to sustaining our humanity.* Routledge.

[29] Bennis, W., & Nanus, B. (1985). *Leaders: The strategies for taking charge.* Harper. Row, p. 41.

[30] Levin, I. M. (2010). New leader assimilation process: Accelerating new role-related transitions. *Consulting Psychology Journal: Practice and Research, 62(1),* 56.

[31] Seaman, J. T., & Smith, G. D. (2012). Your company's history as a leadership tool. *Harvard Business Review, 90(12),* 44-52.

[32] Watkins, M. (2004). *Strategy for the critical first 90 days of leadership. Strategy & Leadership, 32(1),* 15-20.

[33] Bradt, G. B., Check, J. A., & Pedraza, J. E. (2011). *The new leader's 100-day action plan: How to take charge, build your team, and get immediate results.* John Wiley & Sons.

[34] Watkins, M. D. (2013). *The first 90 days, updated and expanded: proven strategies for getting up to speed faster and smarter.* Harvard Business Review Press.

[35] Tichy, N. M. (2014). *Succession: Mastering the make or break process of leadership transition.* Penguin.

[36] Watkins, M. D. (2009). Picking the right transition strategy. *Harvard Business Review, 87(1),* 46-53.

[37] Sarros, A. M., & Sarros, J. C. (2007). The first 100 days: Leadership challenges of a new CEO. *Educational Management Administration & Leadership, 35(3),* 349-371.

[38] Ciampa, D., & Watkins, M. (1999). *Right from the start: Taking charge in a new leadership role.* Harvard Business Press.

[39] Sauer, S. J. (2011). Taking the reins: the effects of new leader status and leadership style on team performance. *Journal of Applied Psychology, 96(3), 574.*

[40] Gabarro, J. J. (1987). *The dynamics of taking charge.* Harvard Business Press.

[41] Stybel, L. J., & Peabody, M. (2007). Beware the stealth mandate. *MIT Sloan Management Review, 48*(3), 11.

[42] Gurl, E. & Tat, M. (2017). SWOT Analysis: A Theoretical Review. *The Journal of International Social Research, 10,* 994-1006.

[43] Helms, M. M., & Nixon, J. (2010). Exploring SWOT analysis—where are we now? A review of academic research from the last decade. *Journal of strategy and management, 3(3), 215-251.*

[44] Losada, M., & Heaphy, E. D. (2004). Positivity and connectivity. *American Behavioral Scientist, 47,* 740-756.

[45] Kahneman, D. (2011). *Thinking, fast and slow.* Macmillan.

[46] Feloni, Richard. "Why Warren Buffett considers the deal he made with an 89-year-old woman one of the best of his career". *Business Insider.* May 1, 2015. Retrieved April 13, 2024.

[47] Linder, K. (2012). *The women of Berkshire Hathaway : lessons from Warren Buffett's female CEOs and directors.* Wiley.

[48] Prescott, John. Nebraska Furniture Mart: A pillar in its 80th year. *Omaha World Herald.* Retrieved from: https://omaha.com/special_sections/nebraska-furniture-mart-a-pillar-in-its-th-year/article_ea21b8bd-2258-5938-814d-b5cbca7132c2.html on April 13, 2024.

[49] Buffett, Warren (March 14, 1984). *Warren Buffett's 1983 letter to Berkshire Hathaway shareholders. Berkshire Hathaway.* Retrieved from: https://www.omaha.com/special_sections/nebraska-furniture-mart-a-pillar-in-its-th-year/article_ea21b8bd-2258-5938-814d-b5cbca7132c2.html on April 12, 2024.

[50] *NFM.com retrieved from: https://www.nfm.com/about-us/ on May 20, 2023.*

[51] Buffett, Warren (March 14, 1984). Warren Buffett's 1983 letter to Berkshire Hathaway shareholders. *Berkshire Hathaway.* Retrieved from www.berkshirehathaway.com on April 12, 2024.

[52] Porter, M. E. (1979). How competitive forces shape strategy. *Harvard Business Review, 57(2),* 137-145.

[53] Uzzi, B., Mukherjee, S., Stringer, M., & Jones, B. (2013). Atypical combinations and scientific impact. *Science, 342(6157),* 468-472.

[54] Markides, C. (1998). Strategic innovation in established companies. *MIT Sloan Management Review.*

[55] Sustainable Harvest Model. https://www.sustainableharvest.com/our-model retrieved on January 11, 2024.

[56] Collis, D. J., & Montgomery, C. A. (2009). Competing on Resources: Strategy in the 1990s. *Knowledge and strategy* (pp. 25-40). Routledge.

[57] Collis, D. J., & Montgomery, C. A. (2008). Competing on resources. *Harvard business review, 86(7/8),* 140.

[58] Uzzi, B., Mukherjee, S., Stringer, M., & Jones, B. (2013). Atypical combinations and scientific impact. *Science, 342(6157),* 468-472.

[59] USAA. (n.d.) *About USAA.* Retrieved April 13, 2024, from https://www.usaa.com/about

[60] McChesney, C., Covey, S., & Huling, J. (2012). *The 4 disciplines of execution: Achieving your wildly important goals (Vol. 34, No. 10).* Simon and Schuster.

[61] Bingham, C. B., & Eisenhardt, K. M. (2011). Rational heuristics: the 'simple rules' that strategists learn from process experience. *Strategic management journal, 32*(13), 1437-1464.

[62] Wheelwright, S. C., & Clark, K. B. (1992). *Revolutionizing product development: quantum leaps in speed, efficiency, and quality.* Simon and Schuster.

[63] Browning, R. (1855). Andrea del sarto. *Men and women,* 7-15.

[64] Wheelwright, S. C. (1994). *Leading product development: The senior manager's guide to creating and shaping.* Simon and Schuster.

[65] Horner, P. (2009). Less is more for HP: Hewlett-Packard earns coveted practice prize by transforming management of massive product portfolio. *OR/MS Today, 36*(3), 40+. https://link.gale.com/apps/doc/A202715160/AONE?u=anon~3c398b2&sid=googleScholar&xid=4a4ba8d8

[66] Cameron, K. (2007). Developing a teachable point of view. *Journal of Management Education, 31*(3), 392-404.

[67] *NFM.com* retrieved from https://www.nfm.com/about-us/ on May 20, 2023.

[68] Eisenhardt, K. M., & Sull, D. N. (2001). *Strategy as simple rules* (pp. 107-112). Harvard Business School Publishing.

[69] Collins, J. (2001). Good to great. Random House Business Books.

[70] Edmondson, A. C. (2012). Teaming: How organizations learn, innovate, and compete in the knowledge economy. John Wiley & Sons.

[71] Edmondson, A. (1999). Psychological safety and learning behavior in work teams. Administrative science quarterly, 44(2), 350-383.

[72] Garvin, D. A., Edmondson, A. C., & Gino, F. (2008). Is yours a learning organization?. Harvard business review, 86(3), 109.

[73] Edmondson, A. C. (2013). The three pillars of a teaming culture. Harvard Business Review, 17.

[74] Scharmer, C. O. (2009). *Theory U: Leading from the future as it emerges.* Berrett-Koehler Publishers.

[75] Brown, T. (2009). *Change by design: how design thinking transforms organizations and inspires innovation.* HarperBusiness.

[76] Tichy, N. M. (2009). *The leadership engine: how winning companies build leaders at every level.* Harper Collins.

[77] Kotter, J. P. (2017). What leaders really do. *Leadership perspectives* (pp. 7-15). Routledge.

[78] Hargrove, R. (2011). *Your First 100 Days in a New Executive Job.* Masterful Coaching Press.

[79] Nietzsche, F. (2016). *Götzen-Dämmerung: oder Wie man mit dem Hammer philosophiert.* BoD–Books on Demand.

[80] Kennedy, J. (12 September 1962). John F. Kennedy's address at Rice University. *JFK Library.* Retrieved: May 12, 2024 from: https://www.jfklibrary.org/asset-viewer/archives/usg-15-29-2

[81] Gartenberg, C., Prat, A., & Serafeim, G. (2019). Corporate purpose and financial performance. *Organization Science, 30(1), 1-18.*

[82] Sisodia, R., Wolfe, D., & Sheth, J. (2007). *Firms of endearment: How world-class companies profit from passion and purpose.* Wharton School Publishing/Pearson Education.

[83] Laloux, F. (2014), Reinventing Organizations: A Guide to Creating Organizations Inspired by the Next Stage in Human Consciousness, Nelson Parker.

[84] Quinn, R. E., & Thakor, A. V. (2018). Creating a purpose-driven organization. Harvard Business Review, 96(4), 78-85. https://hbr.org/2018/07/creating-a-purpose-driven-organization

[85] Sinek, S. (2011). Start with why: How great leaders inspire everyone to take action. Penguin Books.

[86] Quinn, R. E., & Thakor, A. V. (2019). The economics of higher purpose: Eight counterintuitive steps for creating a purpose-driven organization. Berrett-Koehler Publishers.

[87] Lips-Wiersma, M., & Morris, L. (2018). *The map of meaningful work: A practical guide to sustaining our humanity.* Routledge.

[88] Ludema, J., Whitney, D., Mohr, B., Griffin, T. (2003). *The appreciative inquiry summit: A practitioner's guide for leading large-group change.* Berrett-Koehler Publishers

[89] Berry, L. L., & Seltman, K. D. (2008). *Management lessons from Mayo Clinic: Inside one of the world's most admired service organizations.* McGraw-Hill.

[90] Porter, M. E., & Lee, T. H. (2013). The strategy that will fix health care. *Harvard Business Review, 91(10)*, 50-70.

[91] Liker, J. K. (2004). *The Toyota way: 14 management principles from the world's greatest manufacturer.* McGraw-Hill.

[92] Monden, Y. (2011). *Toyota production system: An integrated approach to just-in-time.* CRC Press.

[93] Kniberg, H., & Ivarsson, A. (2012). Scaling agile @ Spotify. Retrieved from https://blog.crisp.se/wp-content/uploads/2012/11/SpotifyScaling.pdf

[94] Comfort, L. K., & Kapucu, N. (2006). Inter-organizational coordination in extreme events: The World Trade Center attacks, September 11, 2001. *Natural hazards, 39(2)*, 309-327.

[95] A quote by Kenneth Haigh" (n.d.). theysaidso.com. Retrieved Nov 29, 2024, from theysaidso.com web site: https://theysaidso.com/quote/kenneth-haigh-you-need-three-things-in-the-theater-the-play-the-actors-and-the-a

[96] Collins, J. (2001). *Good to great.* Random House Business Books.

[97] Lips-Wiersma, M., & Morris, L. (2018). *The map of meaningful work: a practical guide to sustaining our humanity.* Routledge.

[98] Wrzesniewski, A., & Dutton, J. E. (2001). Crafting a job: Revisioning employees as active crafters of their work. *Academy of Management Review, 26(2),* 179-201.

[99] Berg, J. M., Dutton, J. E., & Wrzesniewski, A. (2013). Job crafting and meaningful work.

[100] Tims, M., & Bakker, A. B. (2010). Job crafting: Towards a new model of individual job redesign. *SA Journal of Industrial Psychology*, 36(2), 1-9.

[101] Tims, M., Bakker, A. B., & Derks, D. (2013). The impact of job crafting on job demands, job resources, and well-being. *Journal of occupational health psychology*, 18(2), 230.

[102] Edmondson, A. C., & Harvey, J. F. (2018). Cross-boundary teaming for innovation: Integrating research on teams and knowledge in organizations. Human Resource Management Review, 28(4), 347-360

[103] Buckingham, M., & Goodall, A. (2019). *Nine lies about work: A freethinking leader's guide to the real world.* Harvard Business Press.

[104] Quinn, R. E., & Thakor, A. V. (2018). *Creating a purpose-driven organization.* Harvard Business Review, 96(4), 78-85.

[105] Cross, R., Rebele, R., & Grant, A. (2016). Collaborative overload. *Harvard Business Review, 94(1),* 74-79.

[106] Duhigg, C. (2016). What Google learned from its quest to build the perfect team. *The New York Times Magazine, 26.*

[107] Katzenbach, J. R., & Smith, D. K. (2015). *The wisdom of teams: Creating the high-performance organization.* Harvard Business Review Press.

[108] Katzenbach, J. R., & Smith, D. K. (2008). *The discipline of teams.* Harvard Business Press.

[109] Sinek, S. (2011). *Start with why: How great leaders inspire everyone to take action.* Penguin Books.

[110] Buckingham, M., & Goodall, A. (2019). *Nine lies about work: A freethinking leader's guide to the real world.* Harvard Business Review Press.

[111] Abrams, J. (September 11, 2018). Redeem team:How Kobe Bryant led the rebirth of USA Basketball. Bleacher Report. Retrieved on November 27, 2024 from: https://bleacherreport.com/articles/2795121-how-kobe-bryant-led-the-rebirth-of-usa-basketball

[112] Buckingham, M., & Goodall, A. (2019). *Nine lies about work: A freethinking leader's guide to the real world.* Harvard Business Press.

[113] Buckingham, M., & Goodall, A. (2019). *Nine lies about work: A freethinking leader's guide to the real world.* Harvard Business Press.

[114] Edmondson, A. C. (2018). *The fearless organization: Creating psychological safety in the workplace for learning, innovation, and growth.* Wiley.

[115] Duhigg, C. (2016). What Google learned from its quest to build the perfect team. *The New York Times Magazine.*

[116] Edmondson, A. C., & Lei, Z. (2014). Psychological safety: The history, renaissance, and future of an interpersonal construct. *Annual Review of Organizational Psychology and Organizational Behavior, 1(1),* 23-43.

[117] Edmondson, A. C. (2018). *The fearless organization: Creating psychological safety in the workplace for learning, innovation, and growth.* Simon and Schuster.

[118] Frei, F., & Morriss, A. (2020). *Unleashed: The unapologetic leader's guide to empowering everyone around you.* Harvard Business Press.

[119] Dweck, C. S. (2006). Mindset: The new psychology of success. New York: Random House

[120] Price, C. (2024). *The power of fun: How to feel alive again. Dial Press Trade Paperback.*

[121] Edmondson, A. C. (2018). *The fearless organization: Creating psychological safety in the workplace for learning, innovation, and growth.* Wiley.

[122] Dweck, C. S. (2006). *Mindset: The new psychology of success.* Random House.

[123] Edmondson, A. C. (2012). *Teaming: How organizations learn, innovate, and compete in the knowledge economy.* John Wiley & Sons.

[124] Buckingham, M., & Goodall, A. (2019). *Nine lies about work: A freethinking leader's guide to the real world.* Harvard Business Press.

[125] BenedictineCVDL. (n.d.). *Youtube.* How to Build a People-Centered Culture from the Ground Up - Tasty Catering [Video]. https://www.youtube.com/watch?v=EBQ4xHFuhOs.

[126] Collins, J. (2001). *Good to great: Why some companies make the leap... and others don't.* HarperBusiness.

[127] Tomasello, M. (2008). Origins of human communication. Cambridge, MA: MIT Press.

[128] Sahlins, M. (2013). *What kinship is-and is not.* University of Chicago Press.

[129] Sahlins, M. (2013). *What kinship is-and is not.* University of Chicago Press.

[130] Tomasello, M. (2009). *Why we cooperate.* MIT press.

[131] Tomlinson, I. (May 18, 2022). Create a culture that values team accomplishments more than individual successes. *Harvard Business Review Online.* Retrieved on November 27, 2024 from: https://hbr.org/sponsored/2022/05/create-a-culture-that-values-team-accomplishments-more-than-individual-successes

[132] Seppälä, E., and Cameron, K. (2022). The best leaders have a contagious positive energy. *Harvard Business Review, 100(2),* 98-106.

[133] Fredrickson, B. L. (2001). The role of positive emotions in positive psychology: The broaden-and-build theory of positive emotions. *American Psychologist, 56(3),* 218-226.

[134] Cameron, K. (2021). *Positively energizing leadership: Virtuous actions and relationships that create high performance.* Berrett-Koehler Publishers.

[135] Catmull, E., & Wallace, A. (2014). *Creativity, Inc.: Overcoming the unseen forces that stand in the way of true inspiration.* Random House.

[136] Barsade, S. G. (2002). The ripple effect: Emotional contagion and its influence on group behavior. *Administrative Science Quarterly, 47(4),* 644-675.

[137] Davenport, T. H., & Kirby, J. (2016). *Only humans need apply: Winners and losers in the age of smart machines.* Harper Business.

[138] Sullivan, D. and Hardy B. (2021). *The gap and the gain: high achiever's guide to happiness, confidence and success.* Hay House.

[139] Kahneman, D., & Tversky, A. (1979). Prospect Theory: An Analysis of Decision under Risk. *Econometrica, 47(2),* 263-291

[140] Sullivan, D. and Hardy B. (2021) *The gap and the gain: high achiever's guide to happiness, confidence and success.* Hay House.

[141] Wheelwright, S. C., & Clark, K. B. (1992). *Revolutionizing product development: quantum leaps in speed, efficiency, and quality.* Simon and Schuster.

[142] Wheelwright, S. C., & Clark, K. B. (1992). *Revolutionizing product development: quantum leaps in speed, efficiency, and quality.* Simon and Schuster.

[143] Covey, S. R. (1989). *The 7 Habits of Highly Effective People: Powerful Lessons in Personal Change.* Free Press.

[144] Kim, G., & Spear, S. J. (2023). *Wiring the Winning Organization: Liberating Our Collective Greatness Through Slowification, Simplification, and Amplification.* IT Revolution.

[145] Spear, S. J. (2009). *The high-velocity edge: how market leaders leverage operational excellence to beat the competition.* McGraw Hill.

[146] Drucker, P. (2012). Increasing Knowledge Worker Effectiveness. *Measure What Matters To Customers: Using Key Predictive Indicators,* 95-111. Wiley.

[147] Hammer, M. (2001). The superefficient company. *Harvard business review, 79*(8), 82-93.

[148] Price, B. (1989). Frank and Lillian Gilbreth and the manufacture and marketing of motion study, 1908-1924. *Business and economic history,* 88-98.

[149] Kim, G., & Spear, S. J. (2023). *Wiring the Winning Organization: Liberating Our Collective Greatness Through Slowification, Simplification, and Amplification.* IT Revolution.

[150] Spear, S. J. (2009). *The high-velocity edge: how market leaders leverage operational excellence to beat the competition.* McGraw Hill.

[151] Kim, G., & Spear, S. J. (2023). *Wiring the Winning Organization: Liberating Our Collective Greatness Through Slowification, Simplification, and Amplification.* IT Revolution.

[152] Spear, S. J. (2009). *The high-velocity edge: how market leaders leverage operational excellence to beat the competition.* McGrawHill.

[153] Spear, S. J. (2009). *The high-velocity edge: how market leaders leverage operational excellence to beat the competition.* McGrawHill.

[154] Edmondson, A. (1999). Psychological safety and learning behavior in work teams. *Administrative science quarterly, 44*(2), 350-383.

[155] Edmondson, A. C., Kramer, R. M., & Cook, K. S. (2004). Psychological safety, trust, and learning in organizations: A group-level lens. *Trust and distrust in organizations: Dilemmas and approaches,* edited by Roderick Kramer and Karen Cook, 239–272. New York: Russell Sage Foundation, 2004.

[156] Chang, S. C., & Lee, M. S. (2007). A study on relationship among leadership, organizational culture, the operation of learning organization and employees' job satisfaction. *The learning organization, 14*(2), 155-185.

[157] Bass, B. M. (2000). The future of leadership in learning organizations. *Journal of leadership studies, 7*(3), 18-40.

[158] Spear, S. J. (2009). The high-velocity edge: how market leaders leverage operational excellence to beat the competition.

[159] Edmondson, A. (1999). Psychological safety and learning behavior in work teams. *Administrative science quarterly, 44*(2), 350-383.

[160] Edmondson, A. C. (2023). *Right kind of wrong: The science of failing well.* Simon and Schuster.

[161] Edmondson, A. C. (2023). *Right kind of wrong: The science of failing well.* Simon and Schuster.

[162] Kim, G., & Spear, S. J. (2023). *Wiring the Winning Organization: Liberating Our Collective Greatness Through Slowification, Simplification, and Amplification.* IT Revolution.

[163] Spear, S. J. (2009). The high-velocity edge: how market leaders leverage operational excellence to beat the competition. *(No Title).*

[164] Edmondson, A. C. (2018). The fearless organization: Creating psychological safety in the workplace for learning, innovation, and growth. Simon and Schuster.

[165] Gephart, M. A., Marsick, V. J., Van Buren, M. E., Spiro, M. S., & Senge, P. (1996). Learning organizations come alive. *Training & Development*, *50*(12), 34-46.

[166] Buckler, B. (1996). A learning process model to achieve continuous improvement and innovation. *The learning organization*, *3*(3), 31-39.

[167] Kim, G., & Spear, S. J. (2023). *Wiring the Winning Organization: Liberating Our Collective Greatness Through Slowification, Simplification, and Amplification*. IT Revolution.

[168] Goldsmith, M. (2010). *What got you here won't get you there: How successful people become even more successful*. Profile books.

[169] Carucci, R., Millward, M., and Hansen, W. (October 22, 20240). What the Best Leadership Teams Do Right. *Harvard Business Review.*. Retrieved on November 28, 2024 from: https://hbr.org/2024/10/what-the-best-leadership-teams-do-right

[170] Rigby, D., Elk, S., & Berez, S. (2020). The Agile C-Suite. *Harvard Business Review*. https://pathtoagility.com/the-agile-c-suite-hbr-response/

[171] Christensen, C., Raynor, M. E., & McDonald, R. (2013). *Disruptive innovation* (pp. 20151-20111). Brighton, MA, USA: Harvard Business Review.

[172] Finkelstein, S. (2004). *Why smart executives fail: And what you can learn from their mistakes*. Penguin.

[173] White, J. and Pore, J. (1991), "Why New Executives Often Fail", *Management Decision, Vol. 29 No. 7*. https://doi.org/10.1108/EUM0000000000076

[174] Hambrick, D. C., & Mason, P. A. (1984). Upper echelons: The organization as a reflection of its top managers. *Academy of management review*, *9*(2), 193-206.

[175] Hambrick, D. C. (1987). The top management team: Key to strategic success. *California management review*, *30*(1), 88-108.

[176] Geletkanycz, M. A., & Hambrick, D. C. (1997). The external ties of top executives: Implications for strategic choice and performance. *Administrative science quarterly*, 654-681.

[177] Mintzberg, H. (2017). Crafting strategy. In *The Aesthetic Turn in Management* (pp. 477-486). Routledge.

[178] Porter, K., Smith, P., & Fagg, R. (2007). Corporate strategy. In *Leadership and Management for HR Professionals* (pp. 381-411). Routledge.

[179] Porter, M. E. (1997). Competitive strategy. *Measuring business excellence, 1*(2), 12-17.

[180] Drucker, P. F. (2004). What makes an effective executive. *Harvard business review, 82*(6).

[181] Edmondson, A. C., Roberto, M. A., & Watkins, M. D. (2003). A dynamic model of top management team effectiveness: Managing unstructured task streams. *The Leadership Quarterly, 14*(3), 297-325.

[182] Bariso, J. (May 19, 2022). A Respected MIT Professor Said Your Success Will Be Determined by 3 Things. *Inc.com*. Retrieved November 28, 2000. https://www.inc.com/justin-bariso/emotional-intelligence-mit-patrick-winston-how-to-communicate-effectively-how-to-write.html

[183] Watkins, M. D. (2012). How managers become leaders. The seven seismic shifts of perspective and responsibility. *Harvard business review, 90*(6), 64-144.

[184] Meisinger, S. R., & SPHR, J. (2013). Leading Executive Teams. *Developing and Enhancing Teamwork in Organizations: Evidence-based Best Practices and Guidelines*, 182.

[185] McChrystal, G. S., Collins, T., Silverman, D., & Fussell, C. (2015). *Team of teams: New rules of engagement for a complex world*. Penguin.

[186] Hackman, J. R. (2002). *Leading teams: Setting the stage for great performances*. Harvard Business Press.

[187] Lencioni, P. M. (2010). *The five dysfunctions of a team: A leadership fable*. John Wiley & Sons.

[188] Hill, L. A. (2003). *Becoming a manager: How new managers master the challenges of leadership*. Harvard Business Press.

[189] McChrystal, G. S., Collins, T., Silverman, D., & Fussell, C. (2015). *Team of teams: New rules of engagement for a complex world*. Penguin.

[190] Hummel, C. (1994). *Priorities: Tyranny of the urgent*. InterVarsity Press.

[191] Lasseter, J. (1995). *Toy Story*. Buena Vista Pictures.

[192] Clark-Hitt, R., Smith, S. W., & Broderick, J. S. (2012). Help a buddy take a knee: Creating persuasive messages for military service members to encourage others to seek mental health help. *Health communication, 27*(5), 429-438.

[193] Silva, V. (2022). *A Phenomenological Study of Veterans' Perspectives of the Battle Buddy Relationship* (Doctoral dissertation, Adler University).

[194] Watkins, M. D. (2012). How managers become leaders. The seven seismic shifts of perspective and responsibility. *Harvard business review, 90*(6), 64-144.

[195] Seppälä, E., and Cameron, K.. "The best leaders have a contagious positive energy." *Harvard Business Review* (2022): 1-8.

[196] Seppälä, E. and Cameron, K. (April 18, 2022) The best leaders have a positive contagious energy. *Harvard Business Review*. Retrieved on November 28, 2024 from: https://hbr.org/2022/04/the-best-leaders-have-a-contagious-positive-energy?utm_medium=email&utm_source=circ_other&utm_campaign=subben email_weekendeditiontop50&hideIntromercial=true&tpcc=subbenemail&deliv eryName=SUB_Ben_WeekendEditionTop50_20241027

[197] Gist, M. (2020). *The extraordinary power of leader humility: Thriving organizations–great results*. Berrett-Koehler Publishers.

[198] Schein, E. H., & Schein, P. A. (2018). *Humble leadership: The power of relationships, openness, and trust*. Berrett-Koehler Publishers.

[199] Cameron, K. (2013). *Practicing positive leadership: tools and techniques that create extraordinary results*. Berrett-Koehler Publishers.

[200] Cameron, K. (2012). *Positive leadership: Strategies for extraordinary performance*. Berrett-Koehler Publishers.

[201] Hess, E. D., & Cameron, K. S. (Eds.). (2006). *Leading with values: Positivity, virtue and high performance*. Cambridge University Press.

[202] Cameron, K. (2021). Positively energizing leadership: Virtuous actions and relationships that create high performance. Berrett-Koehler Publishers.

[203] Edmondson, A. C. (2012). *Teaming: How organizations learn, innovate, and compete in the knowledge economy*. John Wiley & Sons.

[204] Edmondson, A. C. (2018). The fearless organization: Creating psychological safety in the workplace for learning, innovation, and growth.

[205] Collins, J. (2001). Good to great. Random House Business Books.

[206] Collins, J. (2007). Level 5 leadership. *The Jossey-Bass reader on educational leadership, 2*, 27-50.

[207] Carboni, I., Cross, R., & Edmondson, A. C. (2021). No team is an island: How leaders shape networked ecosystems for team success. *California Management Review, 64*(1), 5-28.

[208] Gardner, H. K. (2015). When senior managers won't collaborate. *Harvard Business Review, 93*, 75-85.

[209] Uzzi, B., & Dunlap, S. (2005). How to build your network. *Harvard business review, 83*(12), 53.

[210] Quinn, R. E., & Thakor, A. V. (2019). *The economics of higher purpose: Eight counterintuitive steps for creating a purpose-driven organization.* Berrett-Koehler Publishers.

[211] Collins, J. (2001). *Good to great: Why some companies make the leap... and others don't.* HarperBusiness.

[212] Collins, J. (2001). *Good to great: Why some companies make the leap... and others don't.* HarperBusiness.

[213] Marine Corps Recruiting Slogan, Retrieved from https://web.archive.org/web/20090212095259/http://www.marines.mil/units/hqmc/Pages/2007/PRESS25.aspx on October 20, 2024.

[214] Conley, C. (2017). *PEAK: How great companies get their mojo from Maslow revised and updated.* John Wiley & Sons.

[215] Creating a culture that values team accomplishments, *Harvard Business Review.* retrieved on October 20, 2024. https://hbr.org/sponsored/2022/05/create-a-culture-that-values-team-accomplishments-more-than-individual-successes

[216] Shapiro, M. (2015). *HBR guide to leading teams.* Harvard Business Press.

[217] Erkutlu, H. (2012). The impact of organizational culture on the relationship between shared leadership and team proactivity. *Team Performance Management: An International Journal, 18*(1/2), 102-119.

[218] Edmondson, A. C. (2012). *Teaming: How organizations learn, innovate, and compete in the knowledge economy.* John Wiley & Sons.

[219] Gratton, L., & Erickson, T. J. (2007). Eight ways to build collaborative teams. *Harvard business review, 85*(11), 100.

[220] Kirkman, B. L., & Shapiro, D. L. (2001). The impact of team members' cultural values on productivity, cooperation, and empowerment in self-managing work teams. *Journal of cross-cultural psychology, 32*(5), 597-617.

[221] McChrystal, G. S., Collins, T., Silverman, D., & Fussell, C. (2015). *Team of teams: New rules of engagement for a complex world.* Penguin.

[222] Edmondson, A. (1999). Psychological safety and learning behavior in work teams. *Administrative science quarterly, 44*(2), 350-383.

[223] Argyris, C. (1977). Double loop learning in organizations. *Harvard business review, 55*(5), 115-125.

[224] Katzenbach, J. R., & Smith, D. K. (2008). *The discipline of teams.* Harvard Business Press.

[225] Maley, J.F., Dabić, M., Neher, A., Wuersch, L., Martin, L. and Kiessling, T. (2024), "Performance management in a rapidly changing world: implications for talent management", Management Decision, Vol. ahead-of-print No. ahead-of-print. https://doi.org/10.1108/MD-07-2023-1162

[226] Gruman, J. A., & Saks, A. M. (2011). Performance management and employee engagement. *Human resource management review, 21*(2), 123-136.

[227] Goleman, D. (2017). *Leadership that gets results (Harvard business review classics).* Harvard Business Press.

[228] Hallenbeck, G. (February 16, 2020). Keep a Promising Career on Track & Prevent Derailment. *Center for Creative Leadership.* Retrieved on November 28, 2024 from: https://www.ccl.org/articles/leading-effectively-articles/5-ways-avoid-derailing-career/

[229] Inyang, B. J. (2013). Exploring the concept of leadership derailment: Defining new research agenda. *International Journal of Business and Management, 8(16),* 78-85.

[230] Roosevelt, E. (1983). *You learn by living.* Westminster John Knox Press.

[231] Mueller, C. M., & Dweck, C. S. (1998). Praise for intelligence can undermine children's motivation and performance. *Journal of Personality and Social Psychology, 75*(1), 33–52. https://doi.org/10.1037/0022-3514.75.1.33

[232] Sandberg, S. (2013). *Lean in: Women, work, and the will to lead.* Random House.

[233] Covey, S. M. R., & Merrill, R. R. (2006). *The Speed of Trust: The One Thing That Changes Everything.* Free Press.

[234] Loehr, J., & Schwartz, T. (2003). *The power of full engagement: Managing energy, not time, is the key to high performance and personal renewal.* Simon and Schuster.

[235] Schwartz, T., & McCarthy, C. (2007). Manage your energy, not your time. Harvard Business Review, 85(10), 63-73.

[236] Nakamura, J., & Csikszentmihalyi, M. (2002). The concept of flow. *Handbook of positive psychology, 89, 105.*

[237] Csikszentmihalyi, M. (1990). *Flow: The psychology of optimal experience.* Harper & Row.

[238] Drucker, P. F. (2017). What makes an effective executive. *Harvard Business Review Classics.*

[239] Kotter, J. P. (2012). *Leading change.* Harvard Business Review Press.

[240] Cameron, K. S., & Quinn, R. E. (2011). *Diagnosing and changing organizational culture: Based on the competing values framework.* John Wiley & Sons.

[241] Brooks, A. C. (2022). *From strength to strength: Finding success, happiness and deep purpose in the second half of life.* Bloomsbury Publishing.

[242] Brooks, A. C., & Winfrey, O. (2023). Build the life you want: The art and science of getting happier. Portfolio.

[243] Clear, J. (2018). *Atomic habits: An easy & proven way to build good habits & break bad ones.* Penguin.

[244] Schroeder, A. (2009). *The snowball: Warren Buffett and the business of life.* A&C Black.

[245] Bezos, J. (2017). 2016 Letter to Shareholders. *Amazon.com, Inc.*

[246] Kaplan, S., & Beinhocker, E. D. (2003). The real value of strategic planning. *MIT sloan management review, 44(2), 71.*

[247] The Agile C Suite, Rigby, Elk & Perez, May-June 2020, HBR https://hbr.org/2020/05/the-agile-c-suite

[248] The Agile C-Suite. *Agile Velocity.* Retrieved on 3 April 2025 from: https://pathtoagility.com/the-agile-c-suite-hbr-response/.

[249] Barrett, F. (2012). *Yes to the mess: Surprising leadership lessons from jazz*. Harvard Business Review Press.

[250] Kim, G., & Spear, S. J. (2023). *Wiring the Winning Organization: Liberating Our Collective Greatness Through Slowification, Simplification, and Amplification*. IT Revolution.

[251] Spear, S. J. (2009). The high-velocity edge: how market leaders leverage operational excellence to beat the competition.

[252] Sinek, S. (2009). *Start with why: How great leaders inspire everyone to take action*. Penguin.

[253] Collins, J. C., & Porras, J. I. (1996). Building your company's vision. *Harvard business review, 74(5),* 65.

[254] Quinn, R. E., & Thakor, A. V. (2019). *The economics of higher purpose: Eight counterintuitive steps for creating a purpose-driven organization*. Berrett-Koehler Publishers.

[255] Bartlett, C. A., & Ghoshal, S. (1994). Changing the role of top management: Beyond strategy to purpose. *Harvard business review, 72(6),* 79-88.

[256] Mackey, J., & Sisodia, R. (2014). *Conscious capitalism: Liberating the heroic spirit of business*. Harvard Business Review Press.

[257] Gartenberg, C., Prat, A., & Serafeim, G. (2019). Corporate purpose and financial performance. *Organization Science, 30(1),* 1-18.

[258] Sisodia, R., Wolfe, D., & Sheth, J. (2007). *Firms of endearment: How world-class companies profit from passion and purpose*. Pearson Prentice Hall.

[259] Collins, J. (2001). *Good to great*. Random House Business Books.

[260] IDEO. 7 Simple Rules of Brainstorming. https://www.ideou.com/blogs/inspiration/7-simple-rules-of-brainstorming?srsltid=AfmBOoo3OCNOhH0eEBsaJD6vx45sRQsw6nvmY0aw NPEy8k-4zDKvu1b3 Retrieved January 1, 2024.

[261] Lips-Wiersma, M., & Morris, L. (2018). *The Map of Meaningful Work: A practical guide to sustaining our humanity*. Routledge.

www.ingramcontent.com/pod-product-compliance
Lightning Source LLC
Chambersburg PA
CBHW021705120626
46545CB00004B/1413